the Dedalus Press

editor John F. Deane

LIVING IN POETRY
Guillevic

The Poet in Preson. No. 1

LIVING
IN POETRY

INTERVIEWS WITH GUILLEVIC

TRANSLATED FROM THE FRENCH
BY
MAUREEN SMITH

DEDALUS

DUBLIN 1999

The Dedalus Press

24 The Heath
Cypress Downs
Dublin 6W
Ireland

from the French of *Vivre en poésie*

ISBN 1 901233 40 5

Cover photograph of Carnac by Maureen Smith

Dedalus Press Books are represented and distributed abroad
by Central Books Ltd., 99 Wallis Road, London E95LN

and in the USA and Canada by Dufour Editions Ltd.
P.O.Box 7, Chester Springs, Pennsylvania 19425

The Dedalus Press receives financial assistance from An
Chomhairle Ealaíon, The Arts Council, Ireland.

Printed in Dublin by Colour Books Ltd.

"I uphold
that interviews require a bit of everything."

Jean de LA FONTAINE

Translator's Introduction

While visiting Dublin a few years ago, Denise Levertov suggested I translate into English Guillevic's *Vivre en Poésie*, a series of interviews published in 1980, and which I had read with great interest at that time. I remembered with admiration Guillevic's many statements in this book about the nature of poetry and his own art of writing. Re-reading these interviews more attentively at a later date, I became increasingly aware of their value, not only as revelations about the work of one of France's finest contemporary poets, but also as documents on twentieth century history as lived by one individual. Guillevic's life spans the greater part of the twentieth century (1907-1997), and his experience of early poverty in Brittany, the hardship and terror that was the people's lot in Paris during World War II, the intricacies of his work as a civil servant and his friendship with so many artists and writers, are of considerable interest.

When I told Guillevic that I was translating this book, he was delighted. A further series of interviews was to take place to cover the period from 1980, but these never materialised. At the time of the present interviews by Lucie Albertini and Alain Vircondelet, Guillevic was 70 years of age. To the end of his life, he was busy with many other things, including writing new poems. He died on March 19, 1997. His wish was to be buried in Carnac, the place of his birth, a land of dolmens and megaliths.

It was Braque who first described Guillevic as a *Breton* poet, and even though he lived most of his adult life in Paris and did not write in the Breton tongue, his diction has at times a rasping, granite-like quality, a characteristic bareness and hardness which are features of the Breton landscape. Inner landscapes are so often shaped by those of one's early childhood, and the texture and images, water and earth of Carnac permeate his poetry.

In his work and in his aesthetic there is a constant refusal of "the beautiful line". He rebelled against a certain kind of fashion-

7

able lyricism, and it was Max Jacob who pointed out in a letter on May 20, 1942, that Guillevic was able to be lyrical and have his feet firmly on the ground, to be light and solid at one and the same time. These qualities, along with Guillevic's sense of the essential, his striving for exactness in the words he chooses, his distilling of language to the bare minimum of words, does not always facilitate the translator's task, for each word is its own universe, open to other worlds and further connotations.

In her translations of Guillevic's poems (New Directions, 1970) Denise Levertov brings out the singular quality of his writing as only a true poet could. She read French with remarkable ease; she had had private lessons as a child, and had lived in the south of France in the early years of her marriage. Living in both England and America gave her a feeling for the texture of the spoken language which comes out in her translations. Several of her renderings of these poems ('Portrait', 'Faces', 'Overture/ Opening', 'Of my Death'), are reproduced here. She was undoubtedly attracted to Guillevic's poetry because in its feeling tone and the sense of line it reminded her so much of that of William Carlos Williams, and in the Introduction to her translations of Guillevic she stated that she would never attempt to translate the work of a poet with whom she did not feel a good deal of affinity. Guillevic himself speaks of Williams, and the importance he gave to silence. Denise Levertov's interest as translator was "to reconstitute the original in such English as I imagine the poet might have used if he wrote in English." Hence she allows herself a certain freedom in some departures and coining of phrases, so that the newly-translated poems become meaningful for the reader.

My own task as translator of these conversations is a more modest one, for the rambling, spontaneous nature of armchair talk does not require the same kind of craftsmanship as the translation of poems which, as well as translations, need to be good poems. I have, of course, encountered many difficulties. One of these is the very simplicity of much of Guillevic's language. With his own experience of translating, and the corre-

8

spondence with some of the translators of his poems, Guillevic was quick to realize that it is sometimes difficult to translate *simple* words and expressions. Another difficulty is that Guillevic's humour is often based on word-play or puns of a literary or cultural bent. Where I have found it impossible to convey these in translation, I have indicated it in a note. A further difficulty has been the absence, in current dictionaries, of certain terms used by Guillevic when speaking of events of his youth, for example the army terminology used when speaking of his military service. These terms are no longer in use, and it was only through the help of some local *anciens combattants* that I was able to find an equivalent.

I admit that I am far from satisfied with my own, literal versions of the poems; but I take pleasure in the knowledge that other more experienced poets will soon make Guillevic's work available to those who are unable to read French, and I look forward to reading John Montague's translation of *Carnac*.

These conversations show that Guillevic was an endearing, fun-loving personality. His immense *joie de vivre*, his pleasure in the company of people and things, his sense of humour, undoubtedly helped him to endure the hardship and misfortune, the ugliness, horror and violence of war, illness and the survival guilt experienced by so many who lost neighbours, friends and family to the camps of war-time Europe. His passionate plea for justice based on his own early knowledge of suffering is present throughout his poetry. His language, in its difficult simplicity and its strongly visual impact, reveals to the reader worlds which were only his to know.

I wish to thank Madame Lucie Albertini Guillevic who gave permission for the publication of these interviews. While visiting her in Paris, I was asked to modify in the translation some of the points which at the time of the original interviews were not known, for example the age of Guillevic's father when Eugène was born, etc. Hence these minor revisions do not correspond to the original text.

My thanks are also due to Catherine Boylan, who was kind

9

enough to read the manuscript while on vacation in France, to my brother Denis Smith who, thanks to his professional training, was able to make many suggestions as to the translations of legal terms with which I am less familiar, and of course to Denise Levertov who read my work while I was staying with her in Seattle in 1995. It was her intention to write an introduction to this translation. One can only remember with immense affection her abiding joy in the accomplishments of a fellow-poet, and her wish to share Guillevic's conversations with other readers.

Maureen Smith
Angers, 23 October, 1998.

• *Living in poetry?*

• When I was a youth, I would go for walks in a great forest in Alsace, at Ferrette, in the company of a friend of my own age, fifteen or so.

We used to look at the plain from a cliff-top in the Jura. Before us stretched a scene like those that people take pictures of. There was something else too.

What was it? A trembling sensation, a call to things greater than those which the photograph would have recorded.

One of us said: eternity.

It was vague, and we wanted to explain it in detail. What could have given us the intellectual and physical sensation of eternity?

Who could situate this landscape in some kind of continuity (also concrete) which would be the immensity of space and especially time?

The best thing we could think of was that a bird would come by once every century and pick up something from this plain in its beak. Even better, it would take away a grain of sand from a beach which was as long as this plain was immense.

This way of imagining things, it would seem, allowed us to see that plain, that forest and ourselves in our true dimension. And that image has been with me all my life.

I think it is contrary to the notion of eternity, because in eternity nothing happens; it's the eternal instant. But what does that matter?

That's what I shall call living in poetry: prolonging the real not by the fantastic, the marvellous, images of paradise, but by trying to live what is concrete in its true dimension, living one's daily life in what one might call, perhaps, the epic of the real.

To define the verb to live would be a whole philosophy. And nothing at all.

We can amuse ourselves defining poetry, but we do not define

11

sensations.

A definition cannot convey the sensation of cold to someone who has never known what cold is.

And living is a sensation.

So is poetry.

We can live in religion, in busy-ness, in indifference, in boredom. We can live in hatred just as we can live in love.

We all find our poetry as best we can, as circumstances have led us to find it, but we cannot live without poetry.

Poetry is what allows us to keep on keeping on.

I think that, to a great extent, suicide bears witness to the loss of poetry within ourselves.

The role of the poet and that of the poem is to help the other to find his or her own poetry, and manage to live life in that presence to the self and to things in the course of the most ordinary daily tasks: making coffee alone in the kitchen in the morning, going to work, looking at a pigeon going by, or a moving stone...

If we all dared to situate ourselves in our own true circumstances, in what we are obliged to call the immensity of this adventure we know nothing about — because though science teaches us many things, it does not tell us what it is talking about and where what it is talking about happens to be situated —, there would be no mean life, or boredom, or petit-bourgeois naturalism.

Poetry is the sensation of our relationship with the lowliest and the greatest things, a sensation which makes life a perpetual Monteverdi madrigal.

Finding in life — in one's own life — a certain tonality, a certain prolongation, a certain exaltation; living every daily event in the key of eternity, that, for me, is poetry.

• *What is your first memory?*

• My first clear memory is in Jeumont, an industrial city in the North[1], where my father was a gendarme. The town was not very exciting, and we lived in quite awful barracks under police discipline.

It was the time when the officers would turn up at the gendarme's place, and where he would be punished if even a teatowel had been left on a chair. It was very, very military.

I was at pre-school age. My first memory dates from that time. I was three years old. My parents had acquired a new kitchen range, the fire-hole of which was covered by a lid with a fairly long nickel handle.

One afternoon, I was alone in the kitchen — my mother was not keeping an eye on me — and I raised that lid, dropped it, and it broke. Trembling with fear, I waited for my mother.

I remember the atmosphere at Jeumont — strikes, demos, shouts of "We want butter at nine sous," and the climate of violence that it created. I remember my mother's anguish, because gendarmes were often killed.

I also remember that in order to go to school we used to go under an iron gateway, and I had been told : "Through there, it's Hell."

But for me, the event that is clearest in my mind is that of the broken lid, so strong and so perfectly round, broken by me. So my first memory is one of culpability, in a policeman's house, under a tyrannical mother.

I have another memory, a very repulsive one, of that period in Jeumont. I have always found it extremely unpleasant. I would be between three and five when I attended kindergarten, and my classmates, boys like myself, would catch little white worms with long thread-like tails in the school toilets, and make them run over their hands. They used to collect those worms all along the walls of the latrines. I still remember the nausea I felt.

Strangely enough, as an adult I had a dream of levitation, which I do have from time to time. They say that these are dreams of glory (it's very pleasant to fly through the air), and this dream takes place in the playground at the school in Jeumont. On that particular occasion, I didn't get very far, because my trousers got caught on a nail in the wall.

That kind of school playground stayed with me in dreams until I was fifty, but I was no longer a child, because I was wearing trousers!

• *Do you remember the clothes you wore as a child?*

• Until I was quite old, I was always dressed in my father's cast-offs. My mother used to make my trousers and jackets. She had been the village seamstress before she got married. So she would cut out my clothes from old police uniforms. Always cloth that she had to have dyed grey. I remember I never wore a shirt. My mother would make me shirt-fronts so that it would look as if I were wearing a shirt.It would be knotted behind me, but there was nothing under it. I only looked as if I had a shirt, and later, when I went to senior school, I had a kind of tie. I don't remember how other children were dressed when I was at kindergarten, but in the school at Altkirch, from twelve to eighteen, my schoolmates were the sons of the lower middle classes, shopkeepers, teachers...I was poor. I was always the poor boy.

• *Do you have any happy memories of your childhood?*

• That is what I was asking myself as I spoke to you. Happy memories of my early childhood? I have one agonizing memory: I probably had a temperature, and I could see the devil under my bed. My childhood memories are like that, atrocious. But I have one happy memory of the older girl who must have been ten or twelve, who used to take me to school. She would hold my hand. I was probably already attracted to women. I remember what a pleasure it was for me. And I remember her name; she was called Malfait.

It was probably at that time that the adventure began: loving things, loving the world, holding the instant, cultivating joy within myself, in spite of... Living in poetry even before I knew it.

I was not "pampered" if we take into account the poverty of my background, my mother's harshness, my father's indifference. From that stemmed my need to live in solitude, with things, in things.

> The bread of the condemned, the sweat of arm-pits,
> the greasy finger-mark on the window.

> Edging around the cold,
> to care for the rose.

• *So for you, solitude is your first experience?*

• First and long, continuing experience... It lasted not only during the first part of my childhood. It was always there. Until I was twenty, and later.

• *We imagine a small child in a loving relationship with its parents. Were you breast-fed?*

• Yes, so what? I don't remember that. The only loving memory I have is of that little girl holding my hand; she was probably very nice, but no more so than another. She used to hold my hand; she was very gentle.

• *Did your mother never hold your hand?*

• Probably; she would have to, but I don't remember. Neither pleasant nor otherwise. I remember her hands on my cheeks or my buttocks. And I remember the quarrels with my brother who was my elder by three years and with whom I shared a bed.

• *You lived at one and the same time in fundamental solitude and in ... family promiscuity?*

• Yes. And as a child I never had dreams of escape, dreams of paradise. Very early on, perhaps round the age of ten, or even earlier, my dream was to write. Why was salvation there? I do not know.

• *Did you also, early on, feel different from your schoolmates at junior or senior school?*

• There were differences. To begin with I was the son of a gendarme. Then, my eyesight was not good. I wore glasses from the age of eleven, and at that time and in that place it made me a phenomenon. Until then, nobody had realized I had very poor sight. I didn't know that other people saw differently from me. And when I was in Alsace, I had come from elsewhere.

• *From Brittany?*

• I was born in Carnac, which I left at the age of two for Jeumont. From five to twelve I lived in Saint-Jean-Brévelay, in the Morbihan, but summer holidays were spent in Carnac. We used to stay with an aunt; for me it was a great adventure. (During the time we were in Jeumont, we never went to Brittany, for we could not afford such a journey. There had been no increments in gendarmes' pay at that time.)

• *You say that you learned to walk among the menhirs.*

• The menhirs were the public gardens in Carnac. There were no other gardens. And my mother lived on the second floor of a house near the church, in the alley to the smithy leading to the museum. The menhirs of the Ménec are five or six hundred metres away. And that is indeed where I learned to walk. I know because my mother told me...

• *Which is the more vivid memory you have of that time: of the sea or the land?*

• Oh, the land. Saint-Jean-Brévelay is land, heathland. It's not visual for me, but fleshly. The feel of that earth is my higher education.

I knew several schools. The school at the police barracks until the age of twelve; the primary school. I have written a sonnet about my school at Saint-Jean-Brévelay, which was very poor. The windows in our classroom had no panes. It used to rain in the room. There were about twenty of us, boys and girls, while in the school run by the Brothers there would be four to five hundred pupils. I enjoyed learning, I was a good pupil. I used to do arithmetical problems in advance of the set work.

I was not often at home. We had no homework, and so I was free. I kept out of my mother's way as much as I could, and would go off with my friends from the village, those who spoke French. There were not many who did. They were always the same ones. The others would speak Breton, but we were not allowed to. On Thursdays we would roam off into the fields all day long: deep communion with the earth, the grass, the broom and the heath. We used to go paddling in the water. There were what we called rivers: they were really brooks a few yards wide... There was complicity!

We used to go marauding; I have such memories of that! One day I escaped from an Alsatian dog — we were out scrumping apples — and this Alsatian came out of an orchard (it was a grumpy old fellow's dog), and I escaped from it. I ran faster than the dog. I just galloped along. It took me an hour to get my breath back, and I took refuge in the bracken-covered hut I had built in my father's garden. I was so proud!

We used to have all kinds of rites. For example, if one of us wanted to pick a fight with another, he would take up a little soil, or a twig, or a bit of straw, and put it on the other's shoulder. If the other didn't want a fight, he didn't touch it, but if he brushed off the soil or twig from his shoulder, the fight was on. The others would stand round in a circle, and we would fight until the shoulders of one touched the ground. I was eight or nine years old.

• *Did you often look for a fight?*

• Yes. I liked it. We also used to practise collective masturbation. Four, six, eight or ten of us, in a circle under the oak trees or in among the broom. Very early on, at seven, eight or nine years of age. For us it was a kind of mass for boys. I had a sweetheart. Her mother and mine were friends. They used to chatter away together. This little girl and myself would meet, and kiss...I have a very happy memory of her.

Later on, a priest started a football team. He introduced us to the round ball; I used to play full-back, but I was afraid for my eyes.

• *Did you confess to this priest? Did you tell him of your "sins"?*

• My sins of the flesh, of course. I remember one day we went to confession; there were boys on one side and girls on the other. The priest was late. So we lifted up the girls' dresses. But all that was not the main thing!

The main thing, of course, was the fountains. Fountains by the roadside. Fountains of stone and granite with a cross on top; fountains full of green algae and salamanders. Sometimes the water would flow a little. In my sensitivity, that has played a more important part than anything else. The contact with things. Salamanders in the fountain — we didn't catch them. We were afraid of them! It was a legendary animal.

• *What about birds?*

• Birds have played an important part. Not so much the sight, the contemplation, the beauty of birds, as the birds themselves, because we used to catch them. We would set traps and catch thrushes, bullfinches, chaffinches and so on. But the great joy was to find their nests. We would usually go out in a gang; I remember having gone out alone. We would go deep into the thickets, in the bushes, and look for nests. It was like going out treasure-hunting. Of course there would be nests in the trees, such as magpies' nests. We hardly ever climbed up them. Some boys used to, climbers, but not me. We knew the nests : those would be wrens, those chaffinches with speckles on their eggs. I don't remember ever having destroyed anything. We would look, and touch, and leave the eggs. The main thing was to find them. We didn't take the nests.

We had been told, and it's probably true, that birds do not come back to nests that have been violated.

Sometimes the parent birds would fly around us and screech. "This is a pitiless age."

But what joy to find the treasure, the egg, the nest! The secret, hidden thing, there before our eyes.

Some used to hunt down birds with a sling or a catapult.

I never did that.

BOY

There was a time
when the newspaper was a white square
held by the mother above the doorstep
where a child would play.

And outside there would be
all the nests and all the fields,
all the hollow roads under the wind
with their holes for the snakes.
There were the brambles in the pastures

And in oneself a strength
stronger than the wind,

19

for later and for now,
against all that would surely
be needed.

●

It was for his ransom
that he bought him the bread
and to dim his eye
so as not to take too much milk.

— There was leftover bread
that he could not eat —
for he had so much to tell it.

●

We pretend to be sitting at table
and listening.

But we have slipped
beneath the dead leaves
and we brood over the earth.

We can smile at each other
and show our anger about it.
We stroke the leaves
and we tear them apart.

At the slightest grumble
we leave in tears
and we obey.

●

It was better to fight in the fields
than to fret at sundown,
over her smile maybe,
or because of everything there was.

It was better to make sticks of holly branches,
to keep away the dogs
it was better to fight in the broom,
to hit back and hit back hard —

than to go back to the strange pools,
full of reptiles, mud and roots,
and wait to see the setting sun
pouring in something
that looks like blood.

.

Looking for the road to the fairies,
the sleeping girl in the forest of golden thrushes
the nervous caress of the affectionate beast
emerging toward the darkness of the soil of the fields,
the winter wolves to make them say all
of viper seeds, and the palace of wasps.

.

Talking of wolves, it's only for the fight,
shoving your fist right down their throat
to see their eyes go berserk — for it's good to be strong.

.

When the war is far away in the dockyards of the East,
the village boys
work hard in the fields.

Before the evening dew has touched them,
they need to splash in the water
by the leafy hedges.

And they still know how
to cut a bow from them.

But they do not know
how to dissipate their rage.

• *What about girls?*

• We used to think of them a lot. They held a major part in our conversations, our preoccupations. We all thought about the day when we would be able to have a proper relationship with them. At the time, customs were such that we never envisaged that boys and girls might play together. The girls would never have come with us in the fields of broom and on the heath. They were really two separate humanities, but the other one interested us beyond everything.

• *What about things? That oak wardrobe you talk about at the beginning of Terraqué[2] :*

The wardrobe was made of oak
and was not open.

Maybe dead people have fallen out of it.
Maybe bread has fallen out of it.

A lot of dead people
A lot of bread.

• *Is it one particular wardrobe?*

• No. It's a sort of dark wardrobe, oak. Most furniture: wardrobes, breadboxes, chests, beds, whether closed or not, were made of oak. Better-off people had furniture made of walnut or wild cherry.

• *Were there hollows like wooden bowls carved out in the tables?*

• I have seen that on small farms, but it was going out. There were very thick table-mats, hollowed out. I have never seen people eating from them. That was already a thing of the past. But I've seen the communal room: animals and people together. There were plenty like that, the majority in fact. For example in Cloucarnac, where my mother spent her childhood, there was a single room with enclosed beds. The living-room was separated from the stable by the farm animals' hay racks. You could hear them mooing and breathing.

• *When would this be?*

• When I left Brittany in 1919, some houses had inner walls, but the communal room was more usual; strangely enough, the chickens didn't make much noise when they were there.

• *That dark oak wardrobe, "shining piece of furniture polished by the years," which was there, enigmatically, in that one room, what was in it? Why those dead people?*

• Coffin cupboard. It's explained by the white parts. Coded white.

• *Do you remember death   visiting you when you were a child?*

• A woman doctor once told me that if I spoke so much about stones, it's because as a small child I had had a vision of death visiting me. I don't remember.
An image of death? When you live in the country, you see dead bodies all the time. Dead birds, dead animals...But I don't remember the first person I saw dead. I know that I've never liked seeing dead bodies. But when I was a child I didn't think of death.

• *All the same, it's everywhere in* **Terraqué.**

• Yes, but in *Terraqué,* I had come out of adolescence, in name at least! No I was not preoccupied with death. On the contrary, I remember very well that when I was young I found it very difficult to believe that death existed. I experienced myself as eternal. Even now I find it difficult to convince myself. I still think that death will be overcome, that we shall be able to prolong life. I still believe that.

• *You are incarnate in the word, that's a fact.*

• Of course, but I find it difficult to believe in death. It may seem monstruous, but I have written *On my death* to be aware that I existed, to convince myself that I am mortal.

• *It's the double way : convincing oneself that one is mortal, by extending oneself into writing.*

• I live each instant in the instant itself.

24

If she had wanted

as much from me
as I from her,
my earth,

there would have been no
end to our love.

• *Could you try and find a few landmarks to help us to understand how you found your means of expression in poetry?*

• I have told you: I always knew I would write, and I was always interested in the written word: stories, recitations. Recitations were the Fables of La Fontaine: *The Crow and the Fox, The Weasel and the Little Rabbit, The Farmer and his Children* and the lovely fable called *Death and the Woodcutter*. It really impressed me! And also a ten-line stanza by Coppée: *Do the birds hide away to die?* and *The Dream*, a sonnet by Sully Prudhomme:

> The weaver said to me make your own clothes
> ....
> And alone, abandoned by the entire human race
> whose implacable anathema I was dragging everywhere
> ....
> I found lions standing in my way

I found this last line quite extraordinary, and the mixture of the bizarre and the grandiose was a fantastic poetic impression for me!

I know that I then wanted to use the language of

"recitations", maybe because I lived in a part of the world — in France — where French was not spoken. French was for me, at that time, a hieratic language, used by civil servants, persons of standing and in teaching — something which was sacred in my eyes. In the state school, we were not allowed to speak Breton (or to spit on the floor). So these recitations made me discover a still different language: the hieratic in the hieratic. I think that is what attracted me. Quite an elitist conception! There was an ordinary language and a language for an elite. (Of course, at the time, I did not say it was an elite).

Way beyond this French, there was another language, that of the poem. I then felt — I have often used the expression, but my impression dates back to that time — that out of string, wire was made.

The verse-line was the wire.

• *The spoken language that you heard was string, and the verse-lines you were discovering were wire?*

• Yes, the verse-line was a tense language that could not be modified, that could not be broken. Something strong. Like stone. As I have always been attracted to stone, there was a relationship there. Towards the age of eight or nine, I began to write recitations in the manner of La Fontaine. And I continued. I needed that.

• *Did the others know that?*

• No. I used to write for myself. It's only since I retired from the civil service that I have started to talk. As a child, I was always poor, unhappy, persecuted. I did not want anyone to know. And later, as a civil servant in administration, I did not wish to be singled out, either, as a poet.

• *A double life, in fact!*

• Yes, always! It is only now that I dare to assert things. Poets are only forgiven when they have — in a certain measure — done something... acceptable.

• *When you write now, are you convinced that the solitude you built up for yourself is still the same solitude you feed on?*

• What I shall answer is, because often people do not understand this, that it is precisely because I have been well-anchored, deeply-anchored in this solitude, for as long as I can remember, that I am able to be be sociable, fun-loving, amusing. It's because I am not likely to lose my solitude! I never lose it. I am rooted within myself, and however much I may clown around on the outside, my solitude is always there. Always the same; I have the feeling that I have not changed from about the age of eight or nine. And I make bold to say that I am not unworthy of my childhood.

The day when with my friends I broke into the church collection-box to buy sweets and cherries — that was probably not setting a good example! We must have stolen about eight francs. But I am still the child I was. I have found it difficult to take upon myself the lot of an adult. And I'm not very good at it. I still consider myself a boy.

Aragon said to me one day — he did not agree with me and I was arguing with him. It was at a meeting of the national committee of writers. "Listen, Eugene," he said to me, I know you are six, but couldn't you for once be twelve!" I was so moved...

• *Saying you are six is recognizing that you have not lost that childlike virtue of being in the centre of things and being surprised?*

• That's right. Always; I am in the middle. I am not individual in society; I am the middle. It is not at all a matter of pride. I need a centre, and if it's not me, where is the centre? The centre is myself, everything comes out of me. That is why Jean Tortel says that I write God's poems. I see the mountain, I have always felt different from others and a pariah in difference. Physically, first of all: I have no sense of smell, I can't see clearly, I'm not a good runner...

• *Except when you outrace an Alsatian dog !*

• That is an extraordinary event; I wonder however I managed it.   So I was different : the son of a gendarme, not living in the place in which he was born. At the same time, I must confess that I forecast an extraordinary destiny for myself. Not extraordinary in the sense of a fantastic adventure, but a life in which something would happen, on the inside. A life rich in life.

• *A life in poetry?*

• In poetry, perhaps. I wanted to be a sailor. I was not able to because of my eyes. It was a great disappointment to me. Later on, I found myself in Chateaubriand.

• *You say: "Poetry is something else" and you tell us of "another" life.*

• Yes, I knew that something would happen to me and I would not be the last of the last. I despised no-one. I disdained. This is a confession, but if we tell our story we have to be sincere.
Later, in Alsace, I had an accomplice. From twelve to fifteen, a faithful friend. The last time I saw him he had just joined the army... So even if I had an unhappy childhood, it was inhabited. It was not boring. And I used to snuggle up to things around me. Curl up within myself. I had a relationship with things, a blade of grass, a pebble, and everything I write about my relationship with stones:

If one day you see
that a pebble is smiling at you

Will you go and tell?

I have experienced that.

• *If you had not been so unhappy, do you think you would have spent so much time with the blade of grass?*

• My memories are not those of a middle-class Parisian. If I had been that fellow, I would not have had that relationship with the earth and with things.

• *But I am referring to your suffering. Usually children do not have that experience.*

• I don't know about that. To think that something good has come out of evil, I don't know. That life in the country was good. As far as suffering goes, I have not blessed it. I do not like suffering. For me, that was always evil, morally speaking. Suffering is doing wrong. I have always lived for joy. I felt made for communion. I would dream of love, of a communion with someone else. There was always something which shed a halo over everything.

• *Communion, halo: that's religious vocabulary.*

• But for me, finding a bird's nest was sacred... My parents were Catholics. My father did not practise, and my mother was a bigot. As for me, I was a practising Catholic until quite late, for a very long time. I don't know whether I was a true Catholic, because for me, dogma...
But there was a presence. I would live in that presence. Was that faith? Was it poetry? For me it is the same thing. When I

29

broke with the faith, poetry stayed with me, the same.

• *You speak of a presence. What was that? A loving presence,
or the presence of a judge that made you feel guilty again?*

• Both. It is probably in that measure that I was a Catholic.
On simplifying, Christ was love, the Father, the Judge.

There was also the St Francis of Assisi side. But it did not go
very deep: it was things I had learned. On the other hand, I had a
very strong pantheistic sense. It is that much more than what is
called religion. Anyway, Bretons are more animist or pantheist
than Christian. They are not idealists, more like monists; they
find it difficult to separate matter from spirit. The faith of the
Bretons is much more pagan. The cult of fountains. Saint Roche.
It was not just me. But brought up as Catholics, we would take
part, go to the rogations, to mass and confession. I hated confes-
sion. And I did not say half of what was bothering me.

• *For you there was no "state of grace".*

• Not the feeling, no. Right after leaving the confessional,
perhaps. No, religion was not a joy. It was a presence. Later, that
presence remained, without religion. Moreover, I never wrote
anything good whilst I was a believer. While I could say there is
a god there, everywhere, he is in the tree, the tree has no need of
me. There could not be two of us in the centre.Later I read
Nietzsche : "What, there is a god and it is not me?" I would not
have said that to myself quite so simply.

• *Without saying it to yourself, you simply lived it.*

• I think that living God in oneself is the experience of all
poets.

• *Of all those who go back to the beginning.*

• Lucretius, but also Virgil. And what about La Fontaine: isn't he God? And Lamartine? And Hugo? Hugo is God! And Baudelaire? And Rimbaud? Those who do not experience themselves as God are the Parnassian poets, ornamentalists. They "decorate the sides of the vase", Albert Samain has said. But Nerval certainly experienced God in himself, maybe without realizing it. As for Hugo, he probably knew it.

I think that is the deep nature of poetry. At the base of all religions there is a great poem. There is nothing sacred without poetry, just as there is no poetry without the sacred. We might say that every religion is a poem which has been too successful, and because of that it has become paralyzed. The foundation work, the digging, has stopped. Things are given once and for all; only commentary and application are necessary.

Through poetry, we have to take our sustenance from religion, that is to say, everything that people have invested in it, their lives and possibilities. That is the gist of *Inclus* [3.] It's not by chance, either, that a part of *Terraqué* is called *Rites*. There are gestures which are natural to human beings, gestures provoked by feelings: falling to one's knees to adore someone one loves, letting water trickle through one's hands, drop by drop, performing one's ablutions, stroking an object or a human being. Religion has calcified those gestures. The celebrant's gestures must be re-humanised.

> In the dark
> we can light a candle
>
> and sit by it
> as it rests on the table
>
> for the wonderful pleasure
> of watching the flame.

I have suddenly remembered something: I had an operation for appendicitis in 1946, and was rushed off during the night to the Salpêtrière hospital, in the ward run by Professor Mondor, whom I knew. It was a Sunday evening. In the morning of the same day, I had written this poem:

In the depths of blue there is yellow
and in the depths of yellow there is black

Black which stands up
and looks,

and we can't kill it like a man
with our fists.

Throughout the rest of that day, I had a peculiar taste in my mouth, a taste which I attributed to this poem because while I was writing it that taste was there. In fact, it was there to announce the oncome of appendicitis... I was put to sleep. At the time this was still done with chloroform, which really knocked me out. So I had the terrible sensation that it was my poem that was killing me.

When I awoke, I was madly in love with the night nurse. She would say: "Don't move about all the time; you have an ice-pack." It was impossible to overcome my passion!

Hospitals always make me think of the 1914-18 war: the wounded, the disabled. I remember I was out in the fields when the alarm-signal went off in Saint-Jean-Brévelay. We went into the house, and I saw my father leaving in a charabanc. He was shouting "To Berlin! To Berlin!" and singing the Marseillaise.

Yes, my father was shouting "To Berlin!" when he was mobilized. He didn't go any further than Chantilly. He spent the whole of the war at General Headquarters. I don't remember having missed him, but I think my mother became even stricter because of it.

As children, we were not particularly worried about the war. I only wondered what they would put in the newspapers when it was over. (My mother was a reader of the *Petit Parisien* and the

Pays de France.)

My teacher was killed at the beginning of August. He behaved like a brute with me because I wrote badly. He used to make me put my fingers together and hit me very hard with his ruler. When I learned about his death I thought: that's how it is, all those who attack me will be damned.

Yes, I was convinced of this. The revenge of the offended.

• *But you were seven years old...*

• That man used to punish me for nothing. He died. It was a fair punishment. Of course, I was nobody, but I represented something. Attacking me was attacking that thing. I was seven, all right. Children are people.

As for the next teacher, he was very kind. An old lay instructor who liked me and from whom I learned a good deal. So I was not damned, in spite of my mother, in spite of the other teacher.

• *You are often spoken of as being a man of rock, a primitive being. I think you are close to the earth and therefore you possess an earthly power. In that sense, you are invulnerable to evil forces.*

• I believe — I'm telling you this in confidence — that if I am so strongly attached to rationalism, it is partly so as not to fall into mystic earth-worship[4], because I would fall into it very easily. My reason, fortunately, is opposed to it.

• *Your reason is opposed to it, but it leaves a few holes. Fortunately. And you always find the way to the earth, the way to sap and vigour.*

• There is a pathetic or dramatic element which would not exist if I were to give in. It is not to give more tension to what I write that I do this, but I can see the result. I could have been an

33

alchemist.

• *Poetry is a kind of alchemy.*

• Yes, but my reason brings in elements which create the other side of the dialectic. In Sophocles, there is no self-gratification in failure or misfortune. Nor does Oedipus, for that matter, ever compromise himself[5]. It's also for that reason that I left religion aside. Too easy, all that. There should be no complacency towards anything. In politics, I would be an anarchist by temperament, but my reason stood in the way. It has often been said that my poetry is fraternal. I do not seek to be so. I participate. My sensitivity takes part. There is an earthy, mythical side there. My poetry shows solidarity. It is with...

Through militant action, I met people. Rubbed elbows. Especially in the Resistance. To be different, in solidarity there's nothing strange about that. I think that if I have often felt people's hostility towards me, it's because they felt I was different. The word "hostility" is quite strong. An awkwardness. A questioning.

It's probably not just a joke when I say that I am a prehistoric man. I live more in the elements than in society. That's why I'm not suited to psychology or human relations.

The Hungarian poet György Somlyò said to me one day: "You like everyone, but..." It is true that I have had to defend myself from those around me, especially in the civil service. And when I was a soldier! Soldiers have to be all the same, all chums. I could not be a chum, or be alike.

I was never stuck-up, or haughty. I was a good mate. But the others could feel that within myself, I was stand-offish. You cannot write *Terraqué* and be a good pal all the time.

• *Do you think your mother had the slightest inkling of that singularity?*

• I don't know. I don't think so. She felt that I was not hers.

My brother was her favorite. She knew very well that I escaped her, that I wanted to escape her. That I was not her boy. I was very nice-good-obedient, etc. But she could see that there was no true attachment. I was very hypocritical with her, I used to lie. So as not to be beaten, I would play innocent. As my mother was intelligent — it's the only quality she had — she would guess it.

• *She had not guessed that she had reared an ugly duckling?*

• She had perhaps guessed it too well, and that made her afraid. She was not a good woman. She was as ambitious as she was frustrated. She would have liked to have had an education. She used to push my father. She was limited by her bigoted and guilt-ridden conception of religion, but she always wanted to read, and she read everything she laid hands on: popular novels, serial stories in the *Petit Parisien* and the *Echo de la mode*. Always low-brow literature. She was only interested in what I read so as to tell me how indecent it was. Especially concerning Musset's *Rolla*. She could not understand how we were allowed to read such things at school !

• *Were there a lot of books in the house?*

• There were none at all. To tell the truth, there was one: *Sous la hache du bourreau* (Under the executioner's axe). The martyrdom of priests at the time of the separation between Church and State, during the "inventaires" in particular. And, of course, missals and catechism ... and *Almanach Vermont* one year.

• *So as a child you read practically nothing?*

• No. Oh! I remember. A great event. Towards the age of ten, I had ear trouble. My mother took me to the nuns, who gave me some soothing balm and an *Histoire sainte*. It was marvellous! Genesis, Moses, Joshua, who stopped the course of the sun,

Balthazar: *Mane, thecel, pharès!* And Daniel in the lions' den. What an opening! The world took on another dimension. I had discovered epic.

Later, in Ferrette, I had two means of stocking up books: the small library at the school in Altkirch — just a little cupboard — and the parish priest's better-stocked one. I don't know how or when I was led to read *Le Tour de France par deux enfants*, the height of culture and morals under the Third Republic. This interesting book taught me a lot .

As a schoolboy, I read excerpts from Chateaubriand, Jean-Jacques, George Sand, Théophile Gautier and Musset in a collection called "*Les Grands Ecrivains*".

I also remember having reacted to my reading of a *Traité du style* by Antoine Albalat. In my opinion he put too much emphasis on form as opposed to subject. I came across Louis Veuillot on the priest's bookshelves. I must be one of the rare readers of this reactionary writer of the Second Empire.

I read all of Montelambert's *Les Moines d'Occident*; also *Le génie du christianisme*, and Saint Therese of Lisieux's *Story of a Soul*, the Life of Charles de Foucauld, and many lives of the saints and the blessed. When I was fifteen or sixteen, my bedside book was Lamennais' translation of *The Imitation of Christ*.

• *Why did you read?*

• To learn, to discover the world, to discover myself..., for my own edification.

• *Words, as you have written, were already "for knowledge"?*

• I used to whisper them to myself, I would mumble them, but that was not while reading, but apart from it. I liked to live with them. Some of them would obsess me, but I did not pay much attention to the beauty of the phrases. Unless unconsciously. I remember that when I was out walking, I'd say phrases to myself, anything; I would utter one syllable for each step taken and try to guess from the beginning whether it would end on the left or the right foot. This mania has never left me. (There are silent e's!).

My first novel was a sixpenny detective story: *Simon the dog-headed man*. I don't remember for what occasion that was bought for me. It must have been a present from my father. When the police go into the house of Simon, the dog-headed man, to arrest him, the bandit presses a switch, the floor moves, and the policemen fall into a ditch. I used to like that very much

• *Didn't you have any other books?*

• No. Another event: I was sick; I had to lie in bed for about a month, and the customs officer lent me *Les Misérables*. I was fourteen or fifteen. Great reading. Terrific. I still love that book just as much. I re-read it.

• *When did you read?*

• From the age of twelve to the "bachot", at eighteen, I would get up at four in the morning. I would walk about a mile, whatever the weather, snowing or not (in Alsace there is plenty of snow), and I would do two hours' train travel there, and two hours back. Two hours for a twenty mile journey, that's how it was. We would get to Altkirch by seven, where we had an hour's study. In the evening we would leave school in crocodiles, as far as the station, about a quarter past four, except certain winters when there was no coal, and whence, if there was no train, we would later depart, about seven o'clock in the evening. So I got home after eight-thirty, and I used to get up at four...

During those hours on the train, I would learn my lessons and I would read a lot. I remember the delight I took in reading *Les Rêves du promeneur solitaire*! And *Les Nouvelles Méditations*! I had had this book as a prize when I was in the fourth form. What a discovery!

I have told you about the sonnets I learned at primary school. There was also that strange joy I experienced on studying *Athalie* in second year. I literally fed upon:

C'était pendant l'horreur d'une profonde nuit ...   [6]

But the true pleasure of poetry was revealed to me by Lamartine. It was not at all about the play of words. It was a rocking, a flight, melody...*Le Lac, Le Crucifix*.. I spent a lot of time with Lamartine, and dreamt of him. I used to go off into the woods with my book. So as not to be devoured by mosquitoes, I began to smoke...my father's pipe!

But all of a sudden — I remember it because we are going into these things! — and it is something I had never thought about again. You must think I am making it up.

One morning in spring — I can still see that morning — on drawing near to the station at Ferrette, a little station, it was just light. I was reading the *Mémoires d'outre-tombe* or the *Confessions* of Jean-Jacques, and I asked myself this question: how can one tell about one's past? I told myself that if ever I had to tell about what I had just lived through that morning, and what I was living at that very moment, it would be impossible. One would need more than a hundred pages for a quarter of an hour of one's life. No, it was not possible to write about the past. I shall forget what I am living at this moment. I shall forget everything I have just seen, this life, these people, these colours, these shades of colour; no, I shall never tell about my life.

And here I am, doing just that. Anyway, I don't want to reconstruct my life. I remember events, impressions...So why did this idea come to me?

I used to think that all Memoirs are simplified, that one keeps what one wants or what one may. And for me, it's clear, the deepest impression of childhood comes out in the poems rather than in narrative.

The first kitchen range.

It was to replace
the fireplace.

Your childhood fear.
Hell.

These five lines say more about my childhood than anything
I could tell.

In the elementary maths class, I had Domenico Octavio
Mannoni as teacher. He was twenty-three and I was seventeen.
He had found out that I wrote — probably through Nathan Katz
— and he lent me books. He was himself a poet. I still remember
by heart his poem *Grenade*. He had great admiration for Valéry,
and lent me his *Variétés*. But one book he lent me was extremely
important for me, as for many others of my age: it is the
Anthologie de la nouvelle poésie, a large red book published by
Kra. (I later learned that Marcel Arland had collaborated in it.)[7]
It was supposed to start at Nerval and end with poets that were
under thirty at that time. Mathias Lübeck, for example.[8]

So I discovered a new poetry and particularly free verse.What
joy! We could write poems without rhyme or metre. I would
never have dared. One is not a revolutionary alone! Laforgue,
Apollinaire, Claudel, Cendrars, Reverdy and above all Rimbaud!
(Soon after that he became, and always was, the giant one.)
There was neither Aragon, nor Breton, nor Eluard in that book,
but some Dadaists, Tristan Tzara among others.

I found out about Surrealism on reading the Manifesto. I
gave that book back to Mannoni, saying "I can't see what it adds
to Rimbaud, except that it gives him a school."

Before this I had read *Les Fleurs du mal* (bought with the
money I saved on train fares and lunches) because a supervisor
had read *Une charogne* and other "scandalous" poems to us
during the times we were kept in. I also bought poems by Musset
and Verlaine.

So, having read the Kra Anthology, I said goodbye to the
Lamartino-Parnassian purring.

Had so much noise to be made
about a chair?

— It has no part in the crime.

It is old wood
in repose
forgetting the tree —
and its rancour
it is powerless.

It wants nothing more,
it owes nothing more,
has its own busy life,
is sufficient unto itself.

• *If everyone is predetermined by their childhood, that is particularly so for the poet. I think that the poet's inner landscape — I can find no other words to say that — bears a watermark of childhood memories, because that is where there was revelation of the world and the things that are said to be external. It is also where there took place their first easy, strange or curious encounter with language, with words. I am not saying that poets' inner landscapes are limited to the landscape of their place of birth, but I think they play a fundamental role.*

In his Conversations with Picasso, Brassaï records this phrase of the painter, who was seventy at the time: "It has taken me fifty years to be able to draw like a child again." When all's said and done, the artist, writer or painter always tries to get back to images of childhood.

• That is so, and I wonder whether what I am writing at the moment, short poems of two or three lines, corresponds to the feelings and sensations experienced in my childhood, like flashes. I do not write articulated poems, so to speak, any longer.

Had I been born anywhere else than Carnac, I don't know whether I would be any different, but all the same, I think — I leave it to people of greater substance than myself and to psychowhatsits — should they be interested — to say that the fact of being born in a sacred land affects one. It's just as good as being born in Milly...[9]

When one is born in the land of the menhirs — of the megalithic world — those menhirs that belong to a civilization we know nothing about and which dates much further back than the Celts, one is deep in the unknown, deep in mystery.

There is a very fine text by Anatole Le Braz — the Breton Academician poet — who wrote a preface to the book of memories of Carnac by Zacharie Le Rouzic (I knew him: he was curator at the museum in Carnac) where Le Braz — which means 'the great' — recounts that when he arrived in Carnac, the first time, he had a feeling of something sacred.

Now Carnac is spoilt by all those villas, tourism and gas stations, but something remains, and I think that it counted for me, for my child's sensitivity. I do not mean Carnac beach, but prehistoric Carnac.

I have said that I am a prehistoric man. I live in Prehistory. I experienced that when I went fishing in the Isle of Groix, where there are cliffs a hundred metres high, or maybe I exaggerate...there are places where one is alone, among the rocks, where the way down is precarious, especially for me as I get dizzy. I used to go fishing for hours (I find standing painful except when I fish), and I would be alone, completely alone, and when you are fishing (this is what is marvellous about it) you forget about yourself and everything else. You live, you look at the cork bobbing, you follow it and you receive much more than when you know that you are looking.

I used to forget everything, then all of a sudden I would wake up and see myself there: there would be the rocks, the sea, the seaweed, the gulls and myself. I was at home. I felt good.

At Carnac there are no cliffs like there are at Groix, but why

41

did those men who built the menhirs choose Carnac? Why did they stop at that place? Perhaps quite simply because the sea is calm there and there are not many waves. At the far end of the Quiberon peninsula, there's a family beach, says the publicity.

It might be that this place appeared like a haven of grace. The pine trees, the heath...

I knew Carnac when there was not a single villa (at one end, at Por-en-Dro, there was a tiny fishing port with a wooden shack, a bar for the fishermen to have a drink and, at the other end, the Churchill villa, belonging to the Churchill family, and that's all.) Now there are thousands of villas, and rocks are being broken up to make beaches.

At my time of day, we used to catch eels, small fish and crabs from among the rocks. But the sacred dimension of Carnac is something else.

Those miles of pathways of standing stones, beginning with small ones and then becoming larger, and at the end, the cromlech, the great round stone on which, probably, victims were sacrificed. It is thought that these paths were those of a temple. We don't know.

I would go on speaking about Carnac for a long time, but I have written a book of a hundred and fifty pages about this place, and I would only dilute what I have said better elsewhere.

• *So Eugène Alphonse Marie Guillevic, born at Carnac on August 5th, 1907, Breton through and through?*

• Yes, that's one thing we can be certain of! I have not had my genealogy done. Personally, I never knew my grandparents, except for my paternal grandfather whom I saw once, just once, for an hour. He was already very old. He died when he was almost a hundred. We went to see him the day before we left for Alsace. So I was twelve years old. I offered him a sweet, and he replied, in Breton, "I am a brandy bag, not a sweet bag."

My grandfather must have been born in 1829. He had been a soldier for twenty-one years — three times seven — paid as a substitute. Through my great-grandfather, I go back to the eighteenth century. My father was born twenty-three years before me, in 1854, so his father was fifty-five.

I don't know the exact date of my grandfather's death. I remember one day my father said to my mother "My father will soon be a hundred, and I have no news." So he wrote to one of his sisters through the intermediary of the parish priest, because his sisters could neither read nor write, and the reply came back: "Your father died last harvest. He fell down, and crushed his ribs on the corner of a table."

• *Did your parents speak Breton to each other?*

• They would speak Breton when they did not wish my brother and myself to understand. My father loved telling licentious stories to my bigot of a mother and she would be scandalised.

• *Did your father come from a large family?*

• He had six brother and sisters. His family was even poorer than my mother's. My grandfather was the village weaver. He lived in a hamlet, Kerbuzel, in the little village of Ploemel. They had one of those typical little houses, and everyone lived in the same room, including the cow.

When my father was twelve, his father gave him two sous, and my father told me "With that I could go a long way, as long as I didn't go in anywhere."

So he joined up as a ship's boy, in 1897, and went round the world. He told me — oh, my father didn't speak much — but I wanted to ask him questions all the same (there was a great sense of privacy between us) — that he had been through the trial of the Tierra del Fuego, in which ship's boys were made to climb up the masts; then the sailors would whip them with ropes. Only those who could stand it became sailors; those who fell into the water were not up to much! They would be whipped at minus

43

twenty degrees and even less.

Later in 1907, they nearly didn't see him ever again, because he was shipwrecked off Senegal. At that time he was a State sailor, on the *Jean-Bart*; he was doing his military service. They were shipwrecked for forty days on a sand bank. At the time, of course, there was no radio so no news could be given.

As for me, I was "on the way." I almost missed knowing my father, and my father his son. Then all of a sudden he was back.

• *Do you remember your uncles and aunts?*

• On my mother's side, yes. My mother did not allow us to see our relatives on my father's side. We did not go to the family in Ploemel, where of course there was my paternal uncle, who was a castrator of bulls. But I never saw him except when he came to do his job at Saint-Jean-Brévelay. He was the strongest man in the area. When he died, my father inherited his "title".

My uncle was killed in a village one day when he went to bed with a girl. The young people of the village stoned him to death. He was about forty. Stoned to death, near Auray, during the war. I myself saw him coming to castrate the bulls at Saint-Jean-Brévelay. I would see him passing by. He would blow his horn, and I'd know it was my uncle. We were never introduced!

• *How did they show their strength?*

• I have seen my father going in for competitions as to who would lift the heaviest wheel, the heaviest axle-pin of a cart. He was a colossus, and he had no belly. When I was twelve, he used to hold me on his hand and stretch out his arm. My godfather was my cousin, the son of my uncle the castrator of bulls. I never saw him; I was told that he died as a tramp in Nantes. I found all that out bit by bit.

• *What was your mother's maiden name?*

44

• David. I suppose that one of her ancestors had played the part of David in a mystery play. My paternal grandmother was called Kerzehro, my maternal grandmother Madec. Breton names. Mad means "good", Madec, "Littlegood" or "Goodlittle."

• *And Guillevic?*

• Guillevic means "little devil." It's also the name of a famous make of cider in the Auray region. At the café, you can ask for a cider or a Guillevic. It's a local name: it smacks of the soil.

• *As a child, did you go to the Pardons?* [10]

• I went on the pilgrimage to Sainte-Anne d'Auray and I walked up a staircase, about thirty steps, on my knees. I couldn't understand a thing. The crowd was singing "Ave, ave, ave Maria". It was very impressive. I think, but I can't remember exactly, that my mother made me drink a glass of water in which beggars and cripples had dipped their stumps. I have the memory of it, but did I really drink that water? Did I dream about it later? It reminds me of the admirable poem by Tristan Corbière on Sainte-Anne-la-Palud. I also remember the Pardon at Josselin. There was quite a large crowd, and we lost my brother. It took hours to find him.

There was something incantatory and pagan about these Pardons. There was undeniably communion, collective impetus. I have often spoken of celebration in my poems, and the memory of those Pardons is there for some reason.

• *Celebration, precisely. Was there the sense of celebration in your family?*

• No, and I don't remember any feast days at Saint-Jean-Brévelay. There were probably two: the patron saint's feast and the fourteenth of July.

At Carnac, there is a great feast, Saint Cornély. I have learned later that this saint was a great bishop who spread the gospel to part of Brittany. He is the patron saint of horned animals. Two days before the feast, horned animals would arrive in their thousands. They would be everywhere, in the gardens and back yards. There was such a mooing going on, it was powerful. On the day of Saint Cornély, I think it is September 2, all this cattle would be gathered in front of the church, and the Christians behind them. . .

It is at the feast of Saint Cornély that my parents met, on the merry-go-round. Two or three weeks later, they were married. My mother, who was very small, had been captivated by my father's dark eyes, she said! The great feast of Saint Cornély, and the wooden horses....

At Carnac, Saint Columban, who brought the Gospel from Ireland, is venerated also.

• *Wasn't Christmas a feast too?*

• Christmas was important, but as we had no money, we did nothing. We used to get a few sweets. I remember one great Christmas when I had an orange. My first orange. Once, a Parisian lady came on holiday and she left me a pencil-case...

At Saint-Jean-Brévelay, New Year would be celebrated, and it would be pretty awful. Evening after evening we would go round to all the houses of the married policemen of the barracks. I remember that we used to drink mulled wine and we had to behave ourselves.

• *Did you never have a toy?*

• No, never. We used to make little whirligigs, paddlewheels to put in the streams, "tartarelles"...

• *What did you play at when you stayed at home?*

• I was there so very seldom.

46

• *When you went home in the evening what did you do?*

• We would have something to eat and go to bed. There was no electricity.

• *What kind of lighting did you have?*

• Wax candles were for special occasions. Tallow candles. Petrol lamps. "Pigeon" lamps.

• *As soon as the meal was over, to bed!*

• Yes. And in the bedroom, all along the skirting boards, there was mildew.

• *Did you have no friends or people you knew, outside there?*

• My father used to travel around. He knew a lot of people. He told me I had many illegitimate brothers and sisters! My mother used to go to the farms to buy milk, eggs and butter. I would go with her. I would go into a corner and keep quiet. I did not understand anything. Those ladies spoke Breton. Or else, I would go into the yard.
One day, I got the fright of my life. We were in a mill. I put my hand on a strap, and I was pulled over. I went full circle and fell on my feet. Nothing broken. But what a fright!

• *Did you feel that your parents got on well?*

• No. It was very obvious that they did not. All the same I could hear them making love. For a long time my brother and I slept in the same room as them.

• *Your mother was ambitious for you all the same.*

• I think so, because she did not want me to speak Breton, and later she and my father sent me to Altkirch.

• *That was during your stay in Alsace. Did the other gendarmes' sons go to school?*

• Not at Ferrette. I don't remember whether there were any policemen's sons of my age. We no longer lived at the barracks, but in an aparment, at Madame Martin's. I was the only one to go to school. A son of the captain of the Customs Office also went. A little younger than me. We used to travel together.

• *Do you think it was your parents who insisted on your going to school? Didn't the teacher influence them?*

• The teacher at Ferrette? I knew a lot more than he did. He knew some French, but he didn't exist. The teacher at Saint-Jean-Brévelay was far away. I had passed my school certificate at Josselin with a good mark. No, my parents wanted me to learn, and I remember when they introduced me to the principal of the school in Altkirch, he asked "Will he do Latin?", they replied "What use is Latin?" I have always been sorry I did not do it, but it was not my decision.

I went directly into second form. I was twelve years old and had my school cert. So I never did any ancient history. My first class was a maths class. Geometry. The teacher was called Adam. It's amazing how one remembers the names of so long ago.

• *They are not ordinary names: Adam, Malfait. They're easy to remember!*

• I used to like geometry. I think I answered a question during that very first lesson. The teacher said "who can answer?", and I raised my hand.

It was a mixed school. Small classes. In "terminale"[11] there were about twenty of us. In elementary maths there were two of

48

us. There were the children of the lower middle classes of Altkirch and the children of the whole area who came by train.

The train experience was important. I have already mentioned it when speaking about what I read, but there was something else. I used to travel second class: it cost eight francs sixty a month; workmen used to travel third or fourth class. (There were still fourth classes!). In third class it was seven francs twenty-five. I was sometimes in the third class: in these compartments there would only be working men. They would often sing old German songs. Though it was not permitted, they would often go through the second class, and so I was in touch with them.

It was on this train that I met Nathan Katz, the poet. My first poet friend. I must have been fourteen or fifteen.[12]

• *In the Alsace in which you lived at the time, did you feel you were a Breton?*

• When I left Brittany, I was surprised, because I thought that the world was the same everywhere as at home. It was a shock when I arrived at Ferrette and discovered the countryside; the last foothills of the Jura; they are not mountains but hills with magnificent beech forests and also fir trees. There are meadows and lakes. Picturesque. What Carnac was not, fortunately.

I was a stranger, so to speak, but I didn't think anything of it. I only became conscious of the Breton phenomenon, if I may say so, later on. And what is amusing is that the first to have pointed out the Breton side of my poetry was a Norman, Georges Braque : "Your poetry is very Breton", he said to me. Not surprising that a Norman felt that. Like Follain.

• *You never asked yourself about it?*

• No. We were Bretons. Just as others were Picards or Burgundians. In Alsace, I was very conscious of being what the people from that area call "French", and what the French call

"French of the interior". So I was a Frenchman who had the feeling of not belonging to the area. I soon learned Alemannic — because the language of Ferrette, in the Fribourg-Basle-Altkirch triangle, the Sundgau, is not just any old Alsatian tongue, but Alemannic. I could speak it like a native, but I knew very well that I was not from there.

I liked the Rhine very much, and before the building of the Kembs dam which channelled it, it was a wild river. I felt foreign. It now seems surprising, but the question of being Breton was not on the carpet then. One was Breton. Or from the Auvergne. The Third Republic had been successful in the awful task of doing away with the provinces. It had really been successful in this operation carried out against the Girondists[13]. It had made France Jacobite.

That is what Pierre Jakez Helias [14] says : the ambition of the people in Brittany was to learn French well so as to become "someone", to have a place in society. Pierre Jakez spent his childhood in the country, on farms, speaking Breton. He learned French later. As for me, I lived in the village, and my dream was to travel and go on sea voyages...

I later understood that I only like what is at hand, because it is inexhaustible. I would probably have been very unhappy as a sailor. I am not happy when I travel. I hate to see the landscape changing.

> There must be
> another side to these hills,
>
> other lakes, meadows,
> stretches of countryside
>
> and perhaps another light.
>
> Would you know
> better here than there

standing before a tree, alone,
if it were sounding its conscience?

*

To return in the evening too,
to find the path again,
places, the house.

To sit down with the day's burden,
to look, to try

and to find nothing again
but the need to find again.

*

Here too
something happens
in which change is changing itself,
which is almost here.

*

It is here
that everything lulls my cry.

*

Here there is elsewhere.
Elsewhere, the same.

*

On the way back it will be

something of elsewhere to wait for you always

*

I went in everywhere
one could go in.

I went into many rooms.

I stayed there
without destroying anything.

*

Not a single face.

Not even a wall.

*

To go in, was
to look for the place, to leave,
to wander again.

*

And always the air
tastes only of space.

*

Other times.

• *In your work there are passages, one might almost say
"lessons of things", written at different times, on what one learns
at school: metals, geometrical figures, grammar..., as if you felt
the need to bring to the surface, once and for all, what you
learned at school.*

• Primary school was important for me. I have the impression
that I learned nothing else after that. All I know in history and
geography — it's not much — comes from primary school. It
leaves a mark on you. It enters into you.

I am a son of the Third Republic, which, with all its faults and
defects, especially colonialism and centralization, was just the
same a republic and a democracy. At the time there was an
ethical philosophy which can be disputed: masonic ethics, like all
the philosophy of the Third Republic. Civic instruction, espe-
cially.

There was a doctrine, a dominant society. I do not say that it
was good, but there was one.

• *Eugène, tell us about arithmetic, geometry.*

• I used to like, I appreciated, mathematical reasoning, those
purely abstract things. Perhaps it was a way of escaping the
complexity of life. Exercising one's intelligence alone is certainly
a satisfaction beyond all suffering. I found out on my own the
definition of an ellipse; it was in science that I was best: in
biology, physics, chemistry.

In French I was middling. Besides, I never dared to write
personally, except once when I realized at a quarter to eight, that
I had forgotten to do my French homework, and I was supposed
to give it in at eight o'clock. In class we had read the hymn of
Chanteclair to the sun; and our subject was the hymn of the owl
to the night.

This time I took a sheet of paper and let myself go; I hadn't
the time to think about it. I wrote a page and a half. The teacher
could not believe his eyes. He gave me nineteen and a half out of

twenty. I had let myself go writing.

My motto had always been "get a pass mark." I always told myself: "I am a poor child, I must not be outstanding, I must not fail my exams, let's get a pass mark."

When I took my school cert, there were three subjects, and one of them I found particularly interesting. It was the definition of romanticism. I thought: "I do not know the corrector's opinion, let's take the commentary on Corneille". I was certain to have thirteen out of twenty.

Those are reactions of someone poor.

I've just remembered a phrase from my hymn of the owl to the night; the owl says "and when evening comes, I grip with the ferocious joy of an adolescent this bough where I have awaited the night." I needed to be in a hurry to give that in.

To come back to geometry, I was a victim of that famous phrase by Pascal. I always liked Pascal, at that time and later on (he helped me a good deal to lose the faith), but he misled me: I was a victim of his distinction between the spirit of elegance and the spirit of geometry. I believed it, and I said to myself: poetry is the spirit of elegance, let's forget the spirit of geometry.

• *Was writing only poetry for you?*

• Yes, exclusively. Always this language of wire. String language never interested me. There had to be rhythm and tension.

• *Rhythm, tension...you instinctively make language erotic.*

• Very likely! But I have just remembered something which should not be neglected when speaking of the poet and education.

I said that I learned recitations at school, but I have not spoken about church hymns. It's very important. Especially the psalms, which were in Claudelian lines, so to speak. And they had a kind of wild poetry. They are among the things of importance for me. I did not know that it was poetry until I

54

learned about the existence of free verse.

Later, on reading the *Génie du christianisme*, I found that out. Oh! singing vespers as the sun goes down!...There was a poetry there that Chateaubriand describes admirably. No, the *Tantum ergo*, the *Dies irae*, the *De profundis* have not left me indifferent. It is not the same thing as Sully Prudhomme. Even in Latin, we could understand: *Dixit dominus domino meo Sede a dextris meis...*

When I read Claudel, I was not surprised by the form. It was already familiar to me. It was like vespers.

• *Which you went to?*

• Every Sunday during my childhood and adolescence, I attended mass and vespers.

At Ferrette, I was a cantor, and sometimes I would sing vespers solo. I loved that. There were also some little girls who used to listen, among them Marie-Clotilde. I loved singing plain chant. Ferrette is a town of five hundred inhabitants. It is a little church. At Saint-Jean-Brévelay the church is big. . .

• *At the end of the poem* Boy *you write*:

But they do not know
how to dissipate their passion.

Did you ever manage to dissipate it?

• Never. Still haven't quenched it. That mania for living better, living with strength, ridding oneself of all constraint, all slavery. The revolt against one's parents, against school...

• *A revolt which was not apparent because, as you have said, you were good-nice-obedient and...studious.*

• I used to lie all the time. Good? With my mother, of course

I used to lie: my mother instilled guilt into me. Everything I did was bad. I would go in, wash my hands, bend down, and there was something wrong. In her, in her cold blue eyes and her ever-suspicious pointed nose, there was always some unexpressed notion coming through.

That perpetual suspicion was almost metaphysical. I was the incarnation of sin. I lived through the last judgment throughout my childhood. Nothing I could do was innocent. If I picked up a stone, who was it to be thrown at?

I was probably guilty of being there, and being the image of my father. So I played at being an obedient and respectful child. Besides, I was afraid. In the name of religion, my mother had instilled fear into me. I used to think: if I am disrespectful to my mother, I shall be punished. God will avenge her. That's why I dropped everything, mother, God, religion! It lasted a long time. That was the kind of rage I had, and as writing was already a primordial need, I linked that rage and writing.

When I was young, I never considered writing as a possible profession, not even a way of earning my living, no; writing was to get me out, set me up, distance me from all that. My buoy. A desire for revenge.

As my mother had always told me that I would be good for nothing, that I would die on the scaffold, that no woman would ever want me..., I had a desire to wreak revenge on all these blessings, but it was not primordial. True life for me was freeing myself from that life of wretchedness and dependency, and finding "my place and my formula". At the time, one did not speak of a piece of writing, but of a work. Poetry was a clump of grass to hold on to.

• *A clump of grass can fall to pieces.*

• It's better than nothing. My mother guessed my anger. One day in Ferrette, she wanted me to play cards with her. Suddenly, I was overcome, I grabbed the pack of cards and threw them at her! First act of open revolt. I was sixteen, seventeen. I had had enough.

• Isn't that when you started boxing?

• I was fifteen. I felt inferior, I was a stranger, I was no good, I had to defend myself. Boxing gave me self-assurance. I used to practise with my schoolmates. I would read *La Boxe et les boxeurs*. I wasn't a bad boxer. Of course, I had a handicap: my eyesight, but in any event you don't have to see very far in order to box. I defended myself well, and I had a great left hook which was to my advantage, because from that time onwards I was respected at school.

The first time a guy knocked my satchel out of my hands — that often happened — I punched him straight in the face, and our relationship changed. Boxing gave me self-confidence; I would even look for a fight for the sake of it. My relationships with others became relationships of power.

• You were telling us about a friend you had at that age.

• He was called Henri. He was one or two years younger than me. We were always together. We got on very well. Good friends. He did not go to school. He was an apprentice saddler. We would go out for walks together, look at things, especially animals. Around Ferrette it was very beautiful: there was a ruined castle, beautiful forests. And besides, I was in love. He was my confidant; he was also in love with her, but all the same, he shared.

• Your views and your feelings...

• He used to go on little errands for me. He lived almost opposite her. I was a long way away. They lived in Lower Ferrette, and I lived in Upper Ferrette.

• Have you always been in love?

• Yes, how could one live otherwise! I began before the age of eight. I had passing fancies for a few "sylphs"...With Marie-Clotilde it was true love. Till death ...

• *Was she in love with you?*

• At the beginning, she appeared to show that she was. Then I was a very unfortunate lover. She continued her studies at a boarding school abroad. During the winter of 1923-24, we went sledging together. She came close to me. I threw a snowball at her. She leaned her head on my shoulder. She smiled. I was so happy and then...Tubercular meningitis: she died.

Before that, all summer, as she used to take out her younger sister in a push-chair, I would cast an envious look down all the streets in the hope of seeing her. She did not speak to me. Then we seemed to get on. And she died. I was one of those who carried her to the grave.

• *She was the inspiration for some of your finest poems.*

• It was a great love. I still dream of her now. After more than half a century.

• *That was very painful.*

• Not as painful as it might have been because, at the time, I believed that I would meet her in heaven. I was a mystic believer. I used to read the I*mitation of Christ*. I sublimated.

• *Did you kiss her?*

• I wrote about it in *Déjà* :

> Touching only your hand
> could destroy.

One day, she caressed me, touched me...with a bunch of violets.

ELEGY

There were violets
 with which you honoured me

and those that would grow
by chance in the woods,

that wanted to take me
to the land whence the power
of your violets came.

*

When we trembled
against each other in the wood
by the stream,

when our bodies
became ours,

when we each belonged
to ourselves in each other
and together we went on,

it was also the purport of spring
that passed through our bodies
that knew each other.

*

The tender damp earth
where the violets came,

how similar it was
to what we bore.

*

When our entwined fingers
brought the world to us
and entrusted it to us
for all eternity,

we were not false
you know that, but we trembled,
for space had been waiting
for all eternity.

*

I carried you to the earth
in my weary arms.

At the time I thought
that together we were going
to an eternity.

And that you would see me
carry you in my arms
towards that eternity.

*

At the edge of a great wood,
when the sun would come
and speak otherwise
of what we were,

and stretch out before me
the green world,

what did you want me
to do with myself?

*

I would have gone down
to the distant shores
where the dead are laid,

I would have gone down
to the depths of the deep
to be even a shadow
beside your shadow,

but the land is opaque
and knows the dead
only to invade them.

*

I have searched for you

in every expression
and in the absence of expressions,

in all the dresses in the wind,
in all the held-back waters,
in the touch of hands,

in the colour of sunsets,
in the same violets,
in the shadows beneath all the beeches,

in my useless moments,
in time possessed,

in the discomfort of being here,

in the everlasting hope
that there is nothing without you,
in the earth that rises
for the last kiss

in a trembling,
when I can't believe
that you are not there.

I have searched for you
in the abandoned dew,

in the hazel tree keeping a secret
ready to be let out,

in the stream,
it remembers.

In the bleating of the suckling goats,
in the leaves of the hedgerows,
almost like our own,

in the song of the distant cuckoo,
in the undergrowth going
where we wanted to go.

I have searched for you in places
where the vertical wants to lie down.

I have searched for you
where nothing asks questions.
I have searched these places.

I have searched for you
in the song of the blackbird
singing the past amid the future,
in the space it wants to build.
In the light and the rushes
near the ponds where nothing is forgotten.

It is in my joys
that I have found you.

Together we
made the twilight fall

and caressed the bodies
impatient to serve.

*

I have learnt that a dead girl
who fainted and died,
can turn into sunlight.

• As a child, I had thought that, after obtaining my Bac, I
would become an Arts graduate and, thanks to this I could
become a writer. As I had done no Latin, I was unable to do an
Arts degree. So as soon as I obtained my Bac, I thought of doing
a degree in physics and chemistry.

I remember how passionately I studied the elementary bodies.
I felt myself studying matter closely. Nitrobenzine obsessed me
more than *Le Cid*. I was of course fascinated by weight, optics,
the laws of this world. Can we see in that a proof that material-
ism was lying in wait for me?

One thing was certain: I had to earn my living. I applied for a post as tutor at the Strasbourg Academy. As we received no reply, my classmate with whom I studied elementary maths and myself went directly to the Rectorate, where we were told there were no jobs. Boarding schools did not exist in Alsace. So no prefects were required. The waiting lists for tutors were very long!

My parents had made sacrifices to pay for my studies, and also my brother had chosen a manual job (welder). If he had gone on to study, I would have had to leave school earlier. What option was open to me? The civil service. From what I could observe, what I found most pleasing was Registry. At the time, in rural areas at least, Registry, based on law, was considered to be a noble administration. At Ferrette, the Registry Officer was a fine upstanding man who lived a peaceful existence in a beautiful house outside town. He would travel a good deal, did not appear to be over-occupied, and I thought "If I become a Registry Officer, I shall have time to myself." (On this point, I am referring to Giraudoux's *Jérôme Bardini.*)

For a year I prepared the entrance exam by myself. I studied the Civil Code particularly. I passed and in October 1926 I was appointed supernumerary at Huningue, a suburb of Bâle, twenty kilometers from Ferrette. From that point I underwent a hard apprenticeship, for after a few months I was sent as interim administrator of the Registry Offices of the Upper Rhine.

My first experience was as temporary substitute for a Registry Officer who had gone mad, who had not kept his accounts for goodness knows how long. All the files, the registers, were in indescribable disorder and covered in cigar ash. I was barely twenty years old, had only a few months' apprenticeship behind me, and I had to cope. How was I to manage the cash register? How was I to do the accounts? It was quite crazy. There was no-one I could ask for advice. I was alone. I managed. I worked hard.

I had hardly the time to read during that period of my life (or to learn Breton). I was busy the whole time and had to work extremely hard. I would steal moments to read poems or to write.

I used to read *Les Nouvelles littéraires*. The N.R.F. soon became my favourite review .

The notary at Hirsingue was Maître de Dadelsen, Jean-Paul's father; I used to see him often because of my job. I already knew Jean-Paul, as I had met him on "the train": Nathan Katz introduced him to me. I also met his brother whom I came across later, as a pastor in the south of France, about 1950.

The place I lived in was Huningue, a very interesting place for me as I came from a country of solid land, heath or forests. Huningue was a city of noise and smoke. An industrial city belonging to the Bâle-Hirsingue-Saint-Louis group. It always smelt of aniline dyes, even to me, and I have no sense of smell. And then there was the Rhine, the still untamed Rhine. So it was another landscape which I found quite rewarding.

My room was near the station; I could see a boat bridge. At the time the current was tumultuous (it was later planned, so to speak). The port of Bâle for me consisted of huge cranes which impressed me. The traffic in this port was important, poetically, and so was the fact of being alone again at last. My main poet companions at that time were Baudelaire and Rilke, *Das Studenbuch*.

I used to go to Bâle very often with my classmate Pierre Blum; Bâle was a big town, boring enough, but still, big. I had a very moving experience there before I left for the regiment. In 1927 I saw the first great Van Gogh exhibition, in which about a hundred and fifty of his pictures were shown. It had a strong effect on me. Later, I probably distanced myself from Van Gogh, especially under the influence of Cézanne, but at that point it was really something: things possessed in fury.

In November 1927 I went to do my military service. I was sent to Besançon, to the seventh section of clerks and administration workers, C.O.A., those who are called "rice-bread-salt", that is to say the quartermaster's section. As my father was the chief of police in Ferrette, the commander in charge of recruitment wanted to please him by putting his son in the offices, where I was very bored.

I found army life difficult, especially sleeping conditions, the promiscuity. It's not even an interesting human experience. It's awful. You are in touch with all sorts of people who do not show up as they really are. As usual, I was out of place, having lost my social position, for I was neither farm-worker nor cobbler, but a semi-intellectual, and I was not accepted by the intellectuals, who were bourgeois. I was marginal, in spite of myself; it was perhaps useful, all the same.

That was when candidates to be auxiliary interpreters of German were asked for. I applied, was admitted, and was sent to Mayence as quartermaster, where I was just as bored, if not more so. The men who went with girls soon found their way to hospital. I have seen information from French general staff with photographs of girls sent from all over Germany towards the occupied zone. All of them were ill, to contaminate the French army, said the general staff of the Rhine army. The world is full of surprises!

I did have one friend, who also worked in Registry. With him, at least, I was all right, but I was not well in myself. I kept having stomach pains — the food was awful — and I went on the sick list. So it was the infirmary, the military hospital at Mayence, evacuation to Paris to the Val-de-Grâce hospital where I spent several months. I met all sorts of people. The most interesting were perhaps the fellows from the "Af" building, that is to say criminals who were not sent to the army but to the battalions of Africa, and who did not mix with the other soldiers except in hospital. There were also some Legionnaires. Altogether a fine collection of chaps! Quite a few Parisians. The son of a prefect. The worldly son of a sculptor. I remember a peasant by the name of Goosehead who saw me reading books in Gothic characters; one day he wanted to say something to a Madagascan neighbour, so he said to me: " You speak foreign, so explain to him..."

I read a good deal during that period. At the billet I read with considerable amusement magazines of Verlaine and Mallarmé's times. Maybe the *Conférences des Annales*. An anthology could be produced about what was written about them during their lifetime, and it would be a fine example of stupidity and viciousness. Even the Cubists were never the object of such derision.

When I was at the Val-de-Grâce, I bought myself a few books, the poems of André Spire, for example, a poet I always liked (I later met him and I continued to see him until he died at the age of almost a hundred.) I bought Eluard's *L'Amour, la poésie*: it was my first true reading of a book by Eluard. I liked those poems very much.

For my convalescence, I went to the Ganeval barracks in Strasbourg. My father had left Ferrette for that town. He had been appointed sergeant. My father was greatly appreciated. One day, when I was still at school, someone telephoned to say that I had to go back home immediately. The chief inspector of the gendarmerie of Alsace-Lorraine was coming to give my father the military medal.

Another time, he was congratulated by the minister for "brilliant action." From the beginning of the century, arsonists had been rampant in the area; the German police had never identified them, and my father discovered them. They were two relatively upper-class brothers from a neighbouring village. One of them killed his wife and six children during the night preceding the arrest. I also remember that before 1930, at Ferrette, my father would say to me: "You see that man: he's a German agent. He has settled down here, and married a girl he was supposed to have known previously, but it's a cover-up. He's an agent, for sure." At the time I would smile, but it turned out to be true. In 1940 that man was the head of the pro-Hitler party of the region...

After my convalescence I went back to the Val-de- Grâce, where I finished my military service. On my return to civilian life, I was in my twenty-second year, materially independent (though badly-paid). I did not envisage leaving administration, which guaranteed me the means of existence and left me free in body and mind outside office hours. (At least I thought so, because later that did not turn out to be so easy).

I followed Mallarmé's example. I felt I was a poet, I wanted to be a poet. I rejected both Bohemia and utilitarian literature. Of course, my inner life was what I was vowed to, but I managed fairly easily to stop up the well during office hours. It wasn't easy to stop, but how could one do otherwise? In my daily life, I did not present myself as a poet. In everyone's eyes, I was a minor civil servant, a Breton exiled in Alsace, speaking German and Alsatian. I was the only one to know that I had to bear within myself this strangeness that forced me to write. It was like swimming in underground waters, my social life being a periscope. Labyrinths connected me to these underground rivers and, in this kind of inner sea, I had passionate relationships with things. And I continued to live an epic whose end I had no knowledge of, and I did everything possible for it to be my secret.

Moreover, what was I writing? It had nothing to do with anything I knew. I thought it was shapeless. I wanted, I tried, to write a good poem, but I felt so far away from it. Who could have been in that magma of words in which I could not always find my bearings? The road would be long, solitary, arduous, but it was my road, and I would undergo anything to go along that road, and be able to say, at last : here is a poem.

Here I quote Hölderlin :

> But if one day it is given to me to succeed in what is sacred to my heart, the poem, come then, welcome, oh calm of the realm of shadows : one day I shall have lived as gods live. Nothing else was needed.

I went back to interim work in Alsace, in the office of writs in Mulhouse — an enormous office with about a dozen members of staff. As I mistrusted nobody, I was taken in. Several thousand francs were missing from the cash-box, a deficit delicately made during one of my absences. (I had been to Nancy, to take a professional exam to become district collector. I was not pardoned for this missing money).Much later I learned that the two thieves had been found out. They were two office-workers, habitual thieves. Meanwhile, the inspectors' reports in my regard were not very pleasant. (One inspector said I was barely good enough to sell cheese!) And that deficit stayed with me.

I was appointed district collector of taxes at Rocroi in the Ardennes: a very cold, barren land, of wild beauty. A land of schist, a grey land. I lived rent free in a house connected with the job. The work was endless. The tribunal had been set up again, and the book-keepers had been made redundant. I used to work between eight and ten hours per day. I had worked for the registry in Alsace under Germanic legislation; at Rocroi it was quite different.

I was appreciated by the director at Mézières, a man for whom I had great esteem and respect. I sat for the exam to be a draftwriter. I was not admitted because of the Mulhouse deficit. Every month, a tenth of my small wages was deducted.

I was married in September 1930 to a girl from Ferrette, and my first daughter was born in January 1932. Financially I was not well-off at all. The director at Mézières talked to the head of personnel in registry about me. He allowed me to sit for the draftwriting exam. Later, when I passed, he gave me a job near to him in Charleville-Mézières, where I was on his staff for two years. When I passed the exam to become an inspector and editor in general headquarters, I settled in Paris in 1935. I had never thought of living in Paris and, as I was so sure I would not be accepted, I had sat for this exam to please my director who insisted on it.

The move to Paris took place in difficult conditions. My wife had influenza, and so had my second little daughter, and my elder daughter had septicemia. The doctors at Charleville were letting her die. At that time I was travelling between Paris and Charleville. One morning, I took my little daughter on the train with me to the sick chidren's hospital in Paris, where she was treated with mixed vaccinations. It saved her. That is how I began in Paris.

I was appointed to the office which looked after matters of principle and the defence of the rights of administration in the

Supreme Court of Appeal. I was somewhat less busy than I had been up to that point, and, as I had done before, I was determined to find time to read — I had so much to discover — and time to write. I had time in the evening, at night, on Sundays, during the holidays, but as administrative work was often extremely delicate, I could not help thinking about it outside office hours. At that time I had a dream which was decisive concerning the form of my poems, their "lapidary" side. Up to that point, my poems were of varied structures. I dreamt regularly that I was carving the texts of some dense, elliptic lines on the trunks of the beeches in Ferrette, in Schlossberg (When I woke up, I had forgotten the lines). At such a strong request, I gave in. These dreams then granted me armistice.

So, as I was telling you, my time was strictly measured out. Is it for that reason that I have a characteristic which may seem ridiculous — the mania of knowing the right time? I am thankful for the invention of the quartz watch, which allows me to know the official time of the Observatory down to a second. When I can see that there is a difference of five seconds between that time and my watch, I am already ill-at-ease. I have always had this obsession, and it has only become accentuated. It's not that I take myself for some inter-stellar organism!...

At the Ministry of Finance, my office was at the Rue de Rivoli, door D, opposite the State Council clock. We had marble clocks on the mantelpieces. I worked in the noise of the Palais-Royal square.

Each time, at twelve
the clock would say

we could start it all
another day.

• *So you were completely unknown in literary circles when you arrived in Paris in 1935?*

• Of course. I had published a few poems in small provincial magazines. Do you remember the *Hymn to the owl at night*? I had made a poem of it which appeared in *Les Pyrénées littéraires*. Why that magazine? Because I had read an advert in *Les Nouvelles Littéraires* and I sent the poem.

I also published in *La Grive*, a Mézières magazine edited by Jean-Paul Vaillant, and in a bilingual revue in Strasbourg, directed by Raymond Bluchert. I think it was called *La Vache bleue*. I can't check, as I have none of those things left.

However, I had met several Parisians in Altkirch, through Nathan Katz. One of them, René Jourdain, belonged to a large family of manufacturers, one of whose members was a Minister for a long time. Jourdain was about fifteen years older than me, and he was not concerned with industry. He was an aesthete, an art-lover and he liked modern literature. He lived in Paris on the avenue Victor-Hugo, where he had a private house. He would spend his holidays in Alsace where Parisian friends would visit him. That is how I met one of them in Paris: Henri Cotard; (Cotard like the doctor in Proust.) He was an art critic, and it was probably Cotard who took me to the café Bonaparte, where poets would meet, and where I met Jean Follain. It would be 1937. Through Follain I met other poets: René Massat, Méjean, Fombeure, Fernand Marc...We would meet once a week in the basement of the Capoulade — some of these poets and a few others. We were all unknown. The meeting was public; anyone could come. We used to read our work to each other, usually poems. That's where I found my first supporters. And also my first critics, one of whom was particularly violent.

Jean Follain's friendship was decisive for me. He immediately showed an interest in what I was writing, and helped me with his comments. He was very open to others. We usually perceive Follain as closed up on himself. Of course, he had his own world, but he was very receptive. He gave some of my poems to a magazine: *Le Pont Mirabeau* edited by Philippe-Henri Livet, who died during the war. Livet was very enthusistic about these poems, and published them. I think it would be the end of 1938.

One day, Livet told me he had just received an enthusiastic letter from Jean Tortel, a Marseilles poet. He asked: "But who is this Guillevic? Where is he from?" By chance, I found out that Tortel belonged to the same administration as myself, and strange as it may seem, that made me brave enough to write to him! He replied "It is not the Registry that matters, but poetry!" We became friends. It has lasted for forty years.

Follain also had published an eight-page booklet of mine called *Requiem*. (It would seem that I like Church Latin titles: *Requiem, Magnificat.*) This *Requiem*, dedicated to Jules Supervielle (whom I had met meanwhile, as well as Pierre-Albert Birot), appeared in the booklets of *Sagesse*, published by Fernand Marc, under the name of Eugène Guillevic.

At the same time, I had sent poems to Jean Cassou, who edited *Europe*. Poems included in what was to be *Terraqué* (which at the time was called *Argile*.) Cassou had replied to say that he would publish them and, in the month of July 1939, they were in effect announced for the next number. That number was January 1946, *Europe*, new series, in which one can read *Les Charniers*. I have had poems refused. I have not only known success! I am not referring to the *Ode to the Virgin*, sent to Claudel when I was fifteen. I mean a series of poems that are part of *Choses, Terraqué,* and which had been given to Paulhan by Pierre Neyrac, a doctor friend of Charleville-Mézières who had published at Gallimard. Paulhan gave him back the poems, stating that even if they had some good points, they were "terribly lacking in tone, rhythm and presence". The poems were *Assiettes en faïence usées, Bouteilles vides,* etc.

Later during the war, I met Roland de Renéville, poet and critic, because he was a judge in Paris, and his president in chambers had been president of the tribunal in Rocroi. I gave some poems to Renéville who sent them to the *Cahiers du Sud*. They didn't want them. I sent some more, via Blanchard, to Seghers, who was not interested.

I had had more success with Aragon to whom Massat had sent a poem called *A la mémoire de ceux d'Espagne*; it was published in Spring 1939 in *Commune*. I later put it into *Terraqué* under the title *In Memoriam*.

I was not pleased with these refusals, but I never doubted my vocation. I never asked myself whether I was a good for nothing or a genius. I don't ask myself that type of question. I work. I consider that it is my passion. I think I see that my poems hold together just as a cabinet-maker sees whether his wardrobe holds together .

• *Living in Paris, how did you perceive the Surrealist movement?*

• In 1925, I have said, I had read *Le Manifeste du Surréalisme* and a few other parasurrealist texts in the Kra anthology. I had later read, at René Jourdain's, a few magazines, *Le surréalisme au service de la révolution*, I believe. I had been through them, but all that was alien to me.

I later came to believe, rightly or wrongly, probably not very wrongly, that Surrealism was a Parisian phenomenon. We might say more exactly a city phenomenon. It spread to cities other than Paris. I have never liked Breton's prose works or his terrorism, but on a more serious plane, I have never come to believe in automatic writing or the importance given to dreams.

My dreams have always been my enemies. They have always persecuted me. I have far more nightmares than pleasant dreams. In the poem *Art poétique* in *Terraqué*, I pointed out:

It has always been a matter
of taking root.

Being dissipated into dreaming is against my nature. I am surprised at the parallel established between Novalis and Breton. Novalis seems to me to be a man who is trying to see clearly. When I later read Nadja and *Les vases communicants*, etc., I was not enthusiastic; I do not think, and I repeat, that one has to let oneself go into any kind of automatism. One has to use all one's gifts, one's culture — if one has one — one's critical mind, in order to make something which will at once deliver the one who writes and interest other people...

• *But after two or three years' experience, Soupault and Breton left automatic writing.*

• In any case, the so-called "Surrealist" poems remain a mystery to me. I believe profoundly that the important movement of the first quarter of the century was Dadaism. Dadaism is a movement — I am taking up the word I used regarding the *Manifeste du surréalisme* when I was a schoolboy — which has nothing to do with "schools". It is a state of mind to be found in different countries, whereas Surrealism spread out from France to other countries.

Dadaism was the result of war, a profound revolt against war and the abuse of language and lies. Aragon remained a Dadaist. So were Pierre-Albert Birot and Michaux and Prévert. Surrealism was an artefact.

What I appreciated about the Surrealists was not their literary habits nor their aesthetic, but a certain ethics of revolt and love. That I admired. A revolt which took many of them to revolution. And there was the influence of Eluard...

• *Isn't your attitude to Surrealism that of a son of poor people to the sons of the bourgeoisie?*

• It probably is. Moreover, their publications were hardly accessible. I was able to thumb through a few of them at René Jourdain's. He was a millionnaire, it was said at the time. What is more, I was from the country. I should say a word about that one day to Georges Emmanuel Clancier. He was probably in the same situation as I was.

It can be noticed that in the generation of poets that came after Surrealism, there were not many that were really marked by it, neither Ponge, nor Follain, nor Frénaud, nor Audiberti, nor

Tardieu, nor Seghers, nor Armen Lubin. Char is an exception. Mandiargues was a Surrealist after the war.

I consider that Follain was the first to write outside that movement. He was a little older than I was; he began to publish around 1930. Unlike Follain, I believe I wrote against Surrealist writing, to a certain extent. During the Surrealist period, but distinct from it, there were important poets; I am thinking in particular of Claudel, Léon-Paul Fargue, Supervielle, Reverdy and Valéry, of course; there was Rilke, and Ungaretti, for example, abroad; I should also mention Milosz, whom I like very much, and Jean de Boschère, and Max Jacob.

Those who had the greatest influence on me were Reverdy, Supervielle and Milosz. I also liked the little one knew of Saint-John Perse, especially *Eloge*. Those poets were nearer and dearer to me than the Surrealists.

I realize that the generation which comes after our own was more influenced by Surrealism than we were... An anecdote. In July 1940, I spent an evening with Benjamin Péret. He was just out of prison. We were in a restaurant in the rue Campagne-Première. We had found we had hardly anything in common. Everything I liked, he didn't like, especially Mallarmé, Cézanne...

My encounter with Cézanne was extremely important: a profound shock. Cézanne helped me to emerge from my confusion. I had been influenced by Symbolist poetry, from Rimbaud and Mallarmé to Maeterlinck through Laforgue-Charles Cros-Corbière and many others of the "second zone", Ephraïm Michael — Henri de Régnier (first manner) — Moréas — Viélé-Griffin — Stuart Merril... And having started with Lamartine, and undergone the influence of these poets, I was living in a kind of haze which neither Baudelaire nor even Rimbaud helped me to combat at the time.

It was Cézanne who had this decisive influence on me. From the start, I saw Cézanne — and I believe I am not the only one — as a cosmic painter. So (it must be said) Surrealism did not correspond to my profound taste for concrete things — it was too caught up in states of mind. Suddenly, in Cézanne's three apples I came across the world, the earth, the vortex. And then the precision of an ordered, constructed cosmos.

It has just occurred to me that my love for Cézanne coincided with my approach and my adhesion to Marxism. It happened at the same time. This indicates that at that time I had a need to gather myself together, to muster my energies.

When I look back, everything I have done in life has always been for the needs of writing, for my writing. (I have been told that I was not really a communist but an anarchist, and that communism was an alibi for me. That is an exaggeration. But it is true that my adhesion to Marxism corresponded to a need for synthesis, for centering).

Seeing clearly. Bringing about a poem, that is to say a text of the same nature as Cézanne's three apples... Cézanne is still very close to me. I think that by now I have assimilated him, just as I have assimilated Baudelaire, Trakl. That's what happens when you love someone dearly. Cézanne trained me, and Braque completed this experience. I think I rediscovered the great handler of the French language at the same time: La Fontaine. At that same time, I was reading Milosz...[15]

> Worn porcelain plates
> whose white is fading
> you came to our home brand new.

> We have learned so much
> in that time.

Anybody interested in what the General Registry Office was like in my time should read André Theuriet's novel: *L'Affaire Froideville*, which takes place before 1900 and was still true then. A closed world, archaic. I wrote up reports for the Supreme Court of Appeals, on matters at least ten, and sometimes twenty and even thirty years old. Pure law.

Friendships were rare. The world of civil servants, at least that which I knew, was a world undeserving of the criticism it receives. The people are conscientious, honest, but everywhere there is a desire for promotion, and quite impressive rivalry. There is the will for personal advancement through climbing up the hierarchical scale. It is far from exalting. What I did was not exalting either. It was not banal, bureaucratic work, but reports on difficult points of law. Arguments had to be found to uphold the ideas of the civil service even if they were not convincing.

I once had to uphold that an act had been passed on December 31 at 24 hours and not on January 1 at zero hours. It was not so easy ... I had another dossier that was somewhat spicy : it had to be demonstrated that war was not a cataclysm, which is obvious if one refers to the etymology of the word "cataclysm" (flood), but... It had no relationship with real life, except when I was secretary of the commission of foreign stocks and shares. I saw files of the great international companies; I saw capitalism at work.

There were also petty happenings. One day, I went out to help a colleague who had a little shopping to do. I left my hat behind, and the person in charge said I had left my hat so that it would look as if I was there. And he made me change offices.

In that office, I had opposite me a secondary boss who, on sitting down each day would open his file and say : "Back to my vomit."

We had to be there on time and leave on time. At six-thirty in the evening. One of my colleagues began to leave at six-twenty and after a few days, as he was leaving, he ran into his boss who was coming up from the toilet at the very time at which he was leaving. His boss did not say a word. He just looked at him when he said "Goodbye, administrator." And the administrator went back to the toilet and stayed there until my colleague gave in and left at six-thirty...

But I must go back. I have not said anything about my experience as collector at the registry in Rocroi. It is a job which allows you to see how families live. In the first place you have a list of everything that people possess, inheritances, sales. It is known that such and such, who lives austerely, has money. It is not uninteresting to have knowledge of inheritances, to be in contact with small and large fortunes, and with industry. For me, it was a point of departure of Marxist analysis...I was a member of the office who allowed legal aid, that is to say free legal aid, for court cases. And I have seen scenes à la Maupassant, with even more realism. There were four or five of us, members of the bureau, with as president a retired solicitor, and we would listen to the people who were asking for legal aid. They were asked about their reasons for going to court. Unreasonable requests would be refused.

One day, a couple of peasants turned up; real country bumpkins. Forty or forty-five years old. It's difficult to say what age they would be! Daft. It was the woman who was asking for a divorce. She was asked: "What is your motivation?" She answered : "I can't say." We said : "But we have to know the reasons if we are to deal with your request." So she turned to her husband. "Tell them, tell them yourself." The husband was silent. She burst out: "Tell them you go with the animals..."

I could recount more of these anecdotes, but I have already done so more than once, in particular in the interviews I had with Raymond Jean (whose magazine *Sud* has just pubished part). Of course, it happens that we repeat ourselves, either in poems or in what we say. It is bound to happen regarding facts and obsessions. I would like to point out incidentally, that we can find here things that have already been said in the films, — ten I think — that were devoted to me. I can't invent a different life and different preoccupations each time. I insist on respecting truth and a sense of proportion. Like everyone, I attach great importance to childhood and childhood memories, and it is true that the menhirs have had a more important place in my life than the Avenue de l'Opéra.

But let's get back to the civil service, the Registry; I must insist on how much legal documents, and the practice of law and particularly the language of codes (especially that of the Civil Code), have affected me during the stages of my career and

particularly in my work for the Supreme Court of Appeal ,
because I would spend my office hours with the Civil Code. I
lived it — even though this expresion may seem an aberration.

Claudel gives as a perfect example of a French line : *Tout
condamné à mort aura la tête tranchée*[16].That is Claudel's sense
of humour. Yes, the Civil Code is pure prose, a prose that is a far
cry from journalistic hogwash and present-day publicity *"En fait
de meuble, la possession vaut titre"*. . *"L'usufruit est le droit de
jouir d'une chose comme le propriétaire lui-même, à charge d'en
conserver la substance."*[17] It's perfect, and it imprints itself on the
memory. *"Les substitutions sont prohibées..."*[18]

• *In the Civil Code there are very few adjectives, like in
Guillevic.*

• It is a little like the language of proverbs because it has been
worn down by generations. The Napoleonic code dealt with
habitual and customary rights. It is also a code of the language,
the language of all the provinces. Condensed and collected there.
There are extraordinary terms. When a man dies while his wife
is pregnant, a guardian for the child has to designated. Do you
know what he is called? The curator of the womb. Some lan-
guage! The lawmakers of today would not talk like that. "The
irresponsible bid", legislation on the irresponsible bid! There is
some Rabelais in that!

I was also obliged to read the work of jurists, commentators
on the Codes: Merlin, the jurisconsult of Napoleon I, Dé-
molombes, Troplong, and to go back to the Pandects. It was
really complicated.

• *Were there many of you doing this work?*

• In the office of the Supreme Court, there must have been
five of us. At one point I had an office to myself, for in general
there were five or six of us in the same room. After I was
demobbed, I had a sinister little office, a catafalque-like corridor

overlooking the Rue de Rivoli. Of course it was very noisy; I could not work with the window open. I would sometimes go into the office opposite — which overlooked the Carrousel — to get some air and light ; there were three people in that office.

• *Did you ever write a poem during working hours?*

• Yes. I remember the beginning of one of those poems :

From the handle of the door to the snarling waves of the ocean,
from the metal of the clock to the mares in the meadows,
they are in need.

They will never say of what,
but they ask
with the wretched love of the poor who are helpless.

I remember I wrote that between twelve and two. So I had not managed to exclude poetry entirely from my office hours. It would just burst in. It would be enough to see a patch of sky, the flowerbeds of the Tuileries and even just my hand, just a pencil, for communication to be opened with...what ...the poem is trying to attain as it is uttered. That shows I was not entirely there and it was never total eclipse for me.

We had three weeks to a month to write up a report. So I was in no hurry. In general, at that time, I would write in the evening, on Saturday afternoon, on Sunday. Sometimes, as I came home from the office in the evenings, I'd still be plagued by work problems. This lasted from 1935 to 1942.

• *When you gave in the manuscript of Terraqué in 1941, most of the poems in the book had been written during those years.*

• Some of the poems date from the thirties. some were written in Rocroi between 1930 and 1932, such as *Deux Bouteilles vides*:

> That apple on the table,
> leave it until this evening.
>
> After all, the dead won't bite it
> they eat no bread
> they lap no milk.

I have a precise landmark in time, because I can see myself reading it to the wife of the president of the town tribunal. She was my first audience. She had been a teacher at an *école normale*.

• *Do you remember the first poem to give you the joy of seeming, in your eyes, like a finished poem?*

• *Deux Bouteilles vides*, probably. And the joy of my first free verse!

> On washed rocks
> washed again by the waves.

• *Did you keep those lines?*

• No, but they are my first free verse lines! and there is this other one :

> My hands hanging on to the clouds.

• *You never abandoned that one!*

• No, I took it up again in *Du Domaine*, but I wrote it at Ferrette about 1925! I think *Boeuf écorche* was written before *L'armoire était de chêne*.

• How did you write this last poem?

• In the Chanteclair record shop in the Latin quarter, while listening to Manuel de Falla's *Fire Dance*. It's an encounter I find hard to explain. I also wrote many poems at Porte Brunet, where I lived then :

> One, two, three,
> a king was killed by me.
>
> Swallows fly around -
> my daughters are pretty.
>
> One, two, three,
> He's cold and in the ground.

Each poem was really like a birth after a long pregnancy; with the poem came release, and joy. That does not mean the poem was complete. I have always worked at my poems. Some of them have been revised ten or twenty times or even more. I have written poems of twenty lines, of which only two or four remain. Sometimes there is nothing left of the original poem. I believe that as I grow older I modify less, but all the same! When I look at my notebooks they are full of crossings-out.

I am short-breathed. When I write, I do not stop to look for a word, I make a note or I leave a space and I continue. After that I go back to the text and I work. There are texts that I drag along with me for years; one fine day I say to myself "That's it ! I'll keep that one". There are days of grace. I have sometimes re-written old poems — up to ten poems — on the same day.

Many poor lines become something else quite different ; I can give an example. I had written — it's in *Exécutoire* — a poem in which I wanted to give quite simply the sensation of summer; in which the message, as they say these days, was the summer heat. A sensation. It is the most difficult thing to do in poetry, because one can always express an idea, a feeling, but a sensation... I wanted to speak of summer, insects moving, swarming, humming ...I had written : "These insects that work and eat" and I had continued. I knew very well that it was weak. I always work the same way. I never base my work on sonority. (I never try to write a beautiful line, quite the contrary. There are some that I would die to defend). And it is going on deeper into the idea — I don't know whether it can be called a thought — on going deeper into the "thing" that I found "These insects that live on victories". I think it is a synthetically right expression because in nature everything lives and feeds on the victims of their victories. What is amusing is that it appears to be dictated by sounds. For me it is a happy outcome, but the result of chance.

• *When there is music, incantation, is it due to chance?*

• Organically organized chance? If it is pointed out to me, I demolish. I remember that in *Le Temps*, which appeared in *Exécutoire*, I hesitated about cutting out what I considered to be a good line. Finally I left it in. Whenever I read it now, I like it and it moves me:

When water is weighed with the weight of its blissful silence.

I never had the courage to destroy this line. Why ? I don't know; I think that, all the same, it corresponded.

• *What would you have wanted to do?*

• Divide it, break it, so that it would no longer be a beautiful line.

• *You have almost always had a very critical spirit about what you wrote.*

• Yes, at one and the same time I have trust, and I think : "I believe I'm made for that, I believe what I am doing is of interest," but I'm very critical during the work process. Neither do I know how to establish a hierarchy in my poems. Some poems are better than others, they are of more consequence, etc., but I am always critical about each word.

An anecdote: as I didn't read the humanities, Greek and Latin, I am always afraid that a word, the meaning I give to a word in a poem, will be contradicted or deranged by its etymology. That is why, when I gave the manuscript of *Terraqué* to Gallimard, I looked up all the words in an etymological dictionary. I confronted each and every one of them, the wardrobe, oak, all the verbs...because it bothers me when I see someone write, for example, "white rubrics". Rubrics comes from a Latin word meaning red; someone might not know that, but it bothers me. So I look it up; I am not well-informed; I mistrust.

I was recently in Tokyo and I continued to write a series of poems dedicated to the bee. So I wrote :

> On ne dirait plus
> L'abeille picore
> Et pourtant. [19]

I had no dictionary in Tokyo. When I got back, I checked. The verb "picorer" (to peck, to forage for food) was originally applied to the bee. It was made for it. It was later applied to birds. Isn't it curious?

I am always astounded when I read articles in which my knowledge of language is evoked. I do not understand, for I feel that I am very ignorant. When *Terraqué* came out, there was an article by Claude Roy that greatly amused me. He spoke of Cendrars, and Ramuz, I think, and of me, and he spoke of our "awkwardness" in the use of language, we who were not "French". I hope that in over fifty years of writing, I have learnt a little French!

One day a young girl asked me why my vocabulary was poor. It was a good question. I replied that it was because of my biography. The vocabulary in *Du Domaine* is less poor than in

Terraqué. In it I used words that I would never have used earlier on.

Claude Roy said in his article that he could feel the hesitation and trembling at words of someone who is not sure of himself. Perhaps I am more sure of myself now. Although...

> He has sometimes spoken
> louder than himself.

> Forgive me.

• I am sometimes asked how I managed to have my writing published, as I was unknown. Until the war, I never envisaged presenting a collection of poems. There were three reasons for that : my own opinion about what I was writing (it could not interest any editor); the decision I had taken of never publishing at my own expense; the certainty that I was not yet in possession of a real book (I put aside the possibility of publication of a chapbook). So I worked and waited.

That was when the hazards of war had it that I should meet, in December 1939, in the uniform shop of the seventh section of the C.O.A.[20] at Besançon, a writer whom I knew because I had seen his photo (in *Les Nouvelles littéraires* to be exact), and whose work I had read and admired. He was Marcel Arland. He came from Langres and I came from Dôle, from the Quartermaster's offices, and we had both been sent to the Military School of Administration at Vincennes, which had been moved to Bougenais, a suburb of Nantes.

At Dôle I had an excellent companion, André Adler. He was my apartment neighbour. We got on really well : we used to go for walks outside town. Adler was a maths teacher. He was very fond of poetry, and knew German particularly well. He was a

Communist. (He was one of those who introduced me to the Party.) He was an exemplary man of great rectitude. That is how he used all his influence — as he had taken up a position against Munich — to be mobilized. It was Adler who succeeded Jacques Ducour as head of the Université Libre... But I wanted to get out of Dôle, and I had applied to be admitted as well as Adler to attend lectures in the Military School of Administration.

Excuse me for this new digression, but I can tell you in a few words about how I was admitted to this school, when all the others — four or five hundred — were sons of the rich, especially those backed by Lebrun, Daladier or Reynaud. I was unaware that I had been backed by a lieutenant, a colleague in the civil service, who was in charge of preparing the lists of those admitted. He knew who I was, because as inspector of registry, he worked for the commission of transferable securities, of which I was secretary. It was not easy for him to get me in, but he managed it...

So I met Marcel Arland in the army shop and I introduced myself to him. I said "Marcel Arland?" He replied "Yes". I said to him "I know you, I have read you, I admire you." And I explained that I too wrote.

We travelled together from Besançon to Nantes. He was carrying a lot of luggage. I wonder what he would have done without help. At the time he was preparing his *Anthologie de la poésie française* and carrying with him hundreds and hundreds of books. As we were military personnel, we did not, of course, go through Paris, but we changed trains I don't know how many times to get to Nantes. The journey took twenty-four hours.

We spent part of the night at Saint-Pierre-des-Corps. There was snow and frost. We went for a long walk. We talked about poetry. We were not in agreement about everything. He did not like O.V.de L. Milosz as he considered him to be plaintive, and he did not appreciate Eluard as much as I did. When we were in Nantes, we had adjoining beds at first, and then I was moved to the Office section and he was sent to Food Supplies. He was a sergeant, and I was a corporal. He was exempt from fatigues, where I was not. He himself told the tale of how I caught him at the station just he was about to "desert". War time, and he was leaving. He was fed up. And I snared old Marcel !

On Saturdays, if we had been good, we had twenty-four hours' leave. (Once, so as not to miss my leave, as I was on latrine fatigue, and had no brush, I had to pick up the excrement with my hands.) We would go off to spend the evening in Nantes and come back on Sunday evening. I was not always with Marcel, but we saw each other often. We would drink some good Muscadet, and eat well. We used to sleep at the Hotel des Voyageurs.

So we became very good friends. Friends, not only in literature. When he left the school, he was posted to Algiers and I was sent to be head of Intendancy in Paris, because I had been the best of the whole bunch in the Office section. Even the best on the electric battery, even on budget control, and all that because all those gentlemen who had been "backed" had wanted to do personal work, while I understood very well that the captain who was teaching us knew no more than what he was telling us. (One of my colleagues, an *agrégatif*[21] in financial law, had given in a very good piece of work, of which the captain did not understand one word. He gave him eight out of twenty. Thanks to my excellent memory, I wrote out for him the first twenty pages of his lectures, and I obtained twenty out of twenty.) So I was posted to the Ministry of War.

We were then evacuated to Terrasson in the Dordogne. Yet another escapade in which I showed that I was more courageous than I thought I was. The train taking the entire Intendancy direction staff, civil and military personnel, officers, women, children, captains, colonels..., stopped at the station in Chateauroux. There had been an alarm signal and we were being peppered with gunshot from aeroplanes. All these people were getting off the train and running around on the platform. I thought : "They are going to get killed." So I got off the train, and shouted: "Follow me ! Follow me to the underground shelter!" They all came. Nobody was wounded. I was only a

87

beginner!...

And I thought : "What are they going to say?" but no, they did me the honour of choosing me to review the soldiers on July 14, 1940. Well, after the Armistice, I met Marcel Arland again in Paris. He asked me to give him a manuscript for Gallimard, where he had taken up his activities again; I put together the manuscript of *Terraqué* which I modified a little, later, removing a few poems and adding new ones written after the Armistice. Preparing this manuscript helped me to become aware of my own domain.

Marcel Arland took this document to Gallimard's. Once again, Paulhan was not enthusiastic, but Arland battled on... So Paulhan took all the unpublished texts he had to Drieu la Rochelle, his successor as head of N.R.F., and I received an enthusiastic letter from Drieu: "I like your poetry. I am publishing it in the magazine. If you will accept it, I offer you my friendship..."

I hesitated. I knew who Drieu was. I had read him before the war. I knew that he had been a Doriotist[22] and a friend of the Germans. I knew all that, and I could see what he was writing. But André Gide and Paul Eluard had written for his N.R.F. I was tempted to publish, as I had always dreamt of doing, in that magazine. At the time, I thought that poetry was above, or apart from, contingencies, circumstances, or even better, that its very revolutionary force acted against evil, wherever the texts appeared. In certain poems published in N.R.F. this force, in my opinion, was clearly asserted :

> But it is good for the rocks
> to be alone and closed over
> their night work.

> They may know how
> to overcome their fever
> and resist, alone.

My friend Adler, a Communist and a resister from the very first — the same one to whom I submitted my application to join the Party shortly afterwards — advised me to reply positively to Drieu's offer; I listened to him, and went to see Drieu, who welcomed me. I can say that with Drieu, I was as close as anyone can be to an enemy. We both had great affection for each other. He immediately said to me : "You are a Communist"; I replied "I am not a member of the Party, but it's as if I were." He later told me about his wish — late in June 1944 — to join the Resistance. I passed on his request. I was laughed at...

I saw Drieu at his home. We went out together. We went to see *Electra* on the stage. In general, we did not speak about politics. When I reproached him with Nazi crimes, he replied that the Soviets were as bad. He would say that he was a partisan of socialism, but he preferred to go to socialism through Fascism rather than through Bolshevism, because, according to him, Fascism was less hard.

It is certain that Drieu la Rochelle did not know about all the horrors of the Nazi camps and Nazism itself, and it is likely that it was when he found about them that he committed suicide in 1945. His suicide hurt me a lot. I was very fond of Drieu. Naturally, we were enemies. He knew that. I wrote to him one day, quoting a well-known Irish legend. It's about two brothers who fight each other to the death. Two brothers fighting in a stream. They are brothers. They fight. They stop. They embrace. They weep. One has to kill the other. I said to him : this is our story.

Our relationship was never ambiguous. I would say to him : "How were you able to write that?" Because what annoyed me came through with greater force in writing than in what he said.

So that was how, on Marcel Arland's initiative, with the backing of Drieu la Rochelle, the agreement of Paulhan and the decision of Gaston Gallimard, *Terraqué* was published in Autumn 1942, on very poor paper, in about, perhaps, two thousand or more copies, I suppose. They were soon sold. At the time, people read poetry. There were not many books. Besides, in times of horror, we prefer to read poetry...

This book affected and interested people. It also had very hostile critics. "Poetry without grace or music... What a waste of paper! It is not poetry. It is rugged. It is lacking in feeling. It says nothing."

It is true that it is not Lamartine, my first master! This publication brought me some fine friendships and probably also a little self-confidence...to carry on.

> With the fountains at the far end of the land
> we have been.
>
> With the fountains under the algae's weight
> we have been.
>
> — It was against the air
> and probably
> so as to speak no more.

• In *Terraqué*, the presence of fear has often been pointed out. What is the reason for that?

• I can't give a complete answer to that question.

There is the fact, perhaps the hypothesis, that I was born in Carnac, in a sacred part of the world, where of course one is deep in taboo. It would seem, according to some, that Carnac means *ossuary* in I don't know what language. There is the presence of the sea. When I went back to Carnac in 1930 with my father, we went to see the sea at Por-en-Dro, and when he got close — God knows whether my father was theatrical — he murmured to himself : "Oh the slut!" (One must not forget that he had been a sailor.) It is possible that all that was important.

There was also the maternal repression I have already mentioned and the state of the world too. When I was a soldier, at twenty, we did not feel that the world was in such danger, so close to war, but from 1933 onwards it became serious and even very grave: the war in Abysinnia, the war in Spain, the rise of Hitler, different forms of Fascism: it was impossible not to feel anxious.

There were people who lived outside that. For me, it was terribly present. We knew what Hitler was. He had written *Mein Kampf*. We could see the end coming. And it came. That adds up to a lot of things that inspired fear.

Terraqué contains some poems written after the Armistice in 1941-42. During the war, we lived constantly in an atmosphere of horror and terror. I don't wish to speak here of my private life. I don't wish it to appear in these interviews, but the fact is that I loved a woman who was Jewish, who went into hiding, and I never knew whether she was alive or not. Around us we could see people being arrested, and disappearing. We didn't yet know about the horror of the camps, the charnel houses, but we knew about deportation, executions, shooting, massacres. Horror was present all the time. How could one forget it?

We would try, however, to escape this pressure of terror. I was not of those who said that nothing should be published during the war. In my opnion it would be giving satisfaction to the Occupiers, accepting that we had lost, and were on our knees. I was glad that Sartre and Camus put their plays on. It was normal. But when we met, what did we talk about? So-and-so has disappeared, such-and-such...

And then there was something basic that we have forgotten : we were hungry. Really, in Paris we hardly ate anything. During the winter of 1941-42 we had hardly anything but turnips! And also a sausage which came from the country. One day I received a letter from a chap who had done a three week period of reserve with me, in the camp at Valdahon, in 1936. We had sung the *Internationale* together in the barracks. It had created a stir. So this chap I had never written to, wrote to me: "I am thinking of you, I know how hungry people in Paris are; I'm sending you a parcel." Butter, eggs, ham. But it was exceptional. Sometimes I would go to Brittany and bring back a little something. That state of hunger hardly inspired euphoria. It was not the worst thing, but...

• Terraqué *has often been heard as "traqué", tracked down.*

• Yes. I thought of that when I chose this word as title. I chose it because on thumbing through the *Petit Larousse* (from which the term has, moreover, disappeared since the publication of my book), there was both land and sea: terra-aqua. Not many people are familiar with the word. Even Queneau who knew everything asked me what it meant. I too had thought of "traqué".

I remember that old poet, old compared with me at the time, Louis de Gonzague-Frick, a friend of Apollinaire, who published a little review, *Le Lunain,* and whom I met near Alésia. "Dear poet," he said, "how right you are and how tracked down we are."

We were indeed tracked down! I was often afraid, in bombing raids, for example, or when we crossed the line of demarcation carrying tracts or false identity cards...

When I published poems in *L'Honneur des poètes,* Guillevic was soon recognized under the name of Serpières (a pseudonym chosen for me by Eluard who did not consult me. When I told him that Serpières sounded like "serpillière" [floorcloth], he was surprised; he had only thought of stones).

• *Is there a poem in* Terraqué *that you prefer? A poem that surprises you whenever you read it?*

• There are several. As in general I no longer remember the poem when I read it, I say to myself "Not bad! I didn't think I was able to write that at that time!" When I read things of the past, I always think that I have just learned what I know, and I find out that at thirty I was not as stupid as all that! But what I prefer is perhaps the series of *Choses.*

• *Not* Les Rocs?

• Oh, yes, *Les Rocs*! It is probably the best finished series I did in *Terraqué*. There is perhaps just one adjective that I would no longer use : "A sky rotten with blue". Rotten seems to me to come from some kind of abjectness, and indicate a revolt against established beauty. The move from abjectness to political struggle allowed me to become acclimatised — later — to opening out. In short, to move from the love of dead bodies to the exaltation of exaltation. And even from abjectness to a certain Epicureanism. But I like *Les Rocs* and *L'armoire était de chêne*. It is my publicity poem. My advertisement board. The foal of a certain chocolate [23].

I think that *Exécutoire* (Executory) follows on from *Terraqué*. I put them together for a paperback edition. Together they make a book. In *Exécutoire*, it is mainly *Les Charniers* that has attracted attention, whereas I know that there are other good poems there, for example the *Elégies*.

How did I write *Les Charniers*? It was one day in May, 1945, after May 8, when we found out, when we began to find out what had really happened, when we saw the deported people coming back and saw photographs of the death camps. At that time, I often used to go and see Picasso in his studio, in the company of Eluard. Picasso was not yet invaded by the more or less social visits of Americans. That lunch-time, the three of us were alone. We talked. Picasso had been to the station that morning to see the deported arriving... That same evening, I wrote *Les Charniers* straight off. And Picasso painted a canvas, a great panel with a white background which he also called *Les Charniers*. In short, this poem is a crystallization of impressions, experiences and contact with dead things. Probably the memory of the charnel house in the cemetery at Carnac which so much impressed me when I was a child. Let's not forget that my first publication was a *Requiem*, in reality a series of poems about the remains of animals and plants. Up to a certain age — and that can be seen in *Terraqué* — I was in contact not so much with death — the end of life — as with dead things decomposing. They say it is not

93

only Breton, but particularly connected with Carnac. I am no judge.

I sent my poem to Aragon, who published it in the re-print number of the magazine *Europe*. I wonder whether *Les Charniers* is a good example of a political poem, because in the political it is lived in the flesh.

There Nazism is incarnate in rottenness. I was able to live that rottenness because I lived horror. It was horror that took me to the state in which I could write *Les Charniers*.

Yes, even horror can be lived in poetry. That does not mean that poetry attenuates or weakens horror; it may mean that it brings horror to this level, which enables it, lived in poetry, not to be degrading.

The Charnel-house

Walk among the flowers and look :
at the meadow's end is the charnel-house.

No more than a hundred, but in a pile,
insect-bellied, giant-like,
and feet everywhere.

Sex is indicated by the shoes,
their gaze has drained away.

— They too
preferred flowers.

*

At one of the edges of the charnel-house,
lightly in the air and brave,

a leg — of a woman
of course —

a young leg
with a black stocking

and a real
thigh,

young — and nothing,
nothing.

                    *

Linen is not
what rots quickest.

There is some over there
hardened with leaves.

It has the appearance
of flesh to hide flesh still firm.

                    *

How many knew why,
how many died knowing,
how many didn't know why?

The eyes of those who wept
are all the same,

holes in bones
or melting lead.

                    *

They have said yes

to rottenness.

They have accepted,
they have left us.
We have nothing to do
with their rotting.

As far as we can,
we shall separate them,

put them all
in separate holes,

because together they make
too much silence against the noise.

*

If it were not
absolutely impossible

you would say it was a woman
delighted with love
who is going to sleep.

*

When the mouth is open
or whatever is left of it,

they must have sung
or shouted victory,

or their jaws fell
out of fear.

— Perhaps by chance

and the earth went in.

There are places where one does not know
if it's clay or flesh.
And we fear that the earth, everywhere,
 will be the same and stick.

                    *

If only they would become at once
skeletons,

as clean and hard
as real skeletons

and not this mass
 with the clay.

                    *

Which of us would want
to lie down among them

for an hour, an hour or two,
simply for the homage.

                    *

Where is the wound
that replies ?

Where is the wound
 of living bodies ?

Where is the wound —
for us to see it,

for us to heal it?

*

Here
no repose,

here or there, never
any repose

for what remains
for what will remain
of those corpses.

• I left Registry administration in 1942. I was somewhat tired of that solitary, arid work, dealing all the time with abstract matters. Where was life in all that? And besides, promotion was out of the question, and I didn't get on with one of the bosses. So I took the opportunity of being sent to Price Control, which some time later became Economy Control. For three years — my office was in the Rue Miromesnil — I was head of the office of litigation. For the civil servants of this section, I created an anthology of jurisprudence, and I wrote a manual of penal law and criminal procedure. At the Liberation (I had become a member of the Communist Party at the end of 1942), I founded the (Party) cell of the Minister of National Economy.

In November 1945, I was invited to join the cabinet of François Billoux, Communist Minister of the National Economy. I was placed in charge of Economic Control. In January 1946, I followed François Billoux to the Ministry of Reconstruction and I stayed there during the time of Charles Tillon, until March 1947, the date of the overthrow of the government of Communist Ministers. In this Ministry, I was at first *chargé de mission*, then assistant head of Cabinet. I had to deal with all the matters of a legal nature, including writing up laws on war damage, housing and town planning. I worked extremely hard during those years. I had little time to sleep, and none for reading and writing. The experience was interesting, for I saw what it was to be a man of action... and power. I can understand how attractive it can be, and even go to one's head. But I had other things to do. After March 1947, I went on devoting part of my time to the study of economic problems, and Jean Baby, who was then one of the economists of the Party, asked me to become one of these economists. It meant giving up all literary activity, even writing. I could not do it. My irrevocable need was to write. To "write a successful poem". I refused. I argued that someone else could do the same job as me in economy, but nobody else could write my poems.

Meanwhile, in 1946, I think, I had been appointed inspector in the newly-created General Inspection of the National Economy. So in March 1947, I began my work as inspector. It consisted principally of writing up reports and investigations on the situation of the economy. In 1949, Antoine Pinay, who was then my Minister, struck me off the list of seniors because I had signed a motion in favour of the miners on strike. This measure created such a hullabaloo that it was soon abandoned.

I was recruited by Henri Yrissou, General Inspector of the National Economy, and director of the Pinay Cabinet, who suggested I work with him in his department, which was responsible for the coordination of the economic affairs of France and North Africa. I worked in that section from 1949 until the independence of Algeria. It was very time-consuming and very concrete. I delved into all kinds of questions concerning the economy, from metallurgy to citrus fruit, potassium to esparto grass. It concerned facilitating the exportation of North African produce throughout the world, and the importation of French produce into the Mahgreb. And many other things, such as the application of the Marshall plan in North Africa. My section was responsible for representing Algeria, Tunisia and Morocco in the commercial negociations with other countries.

I must comment on one thing: during all those years, I came into no conflict, or even difficulty, with anybody, and here I include senior civil servants and top-ranking colonials, even though my political stance was well-known, and I played, in a sense, the role of an arbiter. My situation was not the same with successive Ministers, because for avowed political reasons, the access to the grade of inspector general was refused me, whereas it had not been refused to any of my colleagues with less seniority.

Moreover, towards 1960, the dies were cast : if I left the Party, I'd be made inspector general. To which I replied : "So you are obliging me to stay in that wretched Party." I'm not sure that the humour of that remark was understood, but that's how I remained an inspector 'til retirement in 1967.

At the Inspection, I was not, unlike my colleagues, seconded to the *igames* [24] — that is to say the regional civil service; as I was considered subversive, I worked in the central section, where I was held at arm's length; my part in preparing policy drafts was far beneath my grade. I had hardly any work, and the year De Gaulle came into power, I was even able to read the complete works of Proust in the office, and I read them slowly, page by page. (I like Proust immensely. He goes with me on all my journeys; I take a volume of the Pléiade edition. I look at the sentences, and at the words. I no longer allow myself to drift.)

So from 1958 onwards, I was a powerless civil servant without a serious occupation; because I was a communist, all promotion was refused me from 1947 to 1967. I then took advantage of a special leave that De Gaulle had decreed to re-situate the colonial civil servants : the members of what were called the great corps of state were allowed to retire at fifty-five with full salary for four years. In 1963, at fifty-six, I took this leave until my retirement in 1967.

• *Did you militate for the independence of Algeria?*

• Like any militant Communist, I climbed a lot of stairs to ask people to sign petitions. In general, I was very badly received. Most French people were for French Algeria, just as they had been for Pétain...When I hear that the French Communist Party did nothing for the independence of Algeria and for peace between our two countries, it makes me laugh a dark laugh, because, of course, it is not true... Here is a poem I wrote at that time :

Among the hills I hardly knew
there die

men from home
whom I did not know

*

Among the hills I hardly knew
there die

men from Algeria
whom I did not know.

*

Whom I did know, perhaps,
through other men whom
I knew a little;

and look for them
in these others.

*

It is of those one encounters
those who still have faces,

That one asks forgiveness
for those who have lost theirs.

• *So you are a poète engagé?   Since before the war?*

• I do not speak of *poésie engagée*. Engaged — encaged. I
detest that word. Engaged in what, in the colonial troops? I
started to write militant poetry, civic poetry, as Frénaud calls it,
in 1938-39. The two poems that appear in *L'Honneur des poètes*
show my stance against war and fascism. (It's the two songs : *La
Ration de vin* and *Les meneurs du jeu.*)

When Eluard asked me for more poems for the second
volume of *L'Honneur des poètes,* my reply was: I have none. It
was at the Liberation that I realized that many of the poems
written during the war were in fact poems of resistance. For
example, *A l'étal de mon père,* dedicated to the memory of Max
Jacob, or even certain *Elegies* such as :

> We have drunk in secret
> from intact glasses
> wine that was maybe
> meant for us.
>
> We have drunk in secret
> among the crowds
> restless in the sun.
>
> It was when we came out of our labyrinths
> and our hands were unsure(.............)

Eluard was very fond of this poem.

It is true that we were so immersed in horror that it came
naturally. As Jacques Duclos said to me: "You know, political
poetry is right for times of horror." After the war, I wrote poems
— certainly not commissioned — nobody ever commissioned

anything from me — but poems published in *Gagner* which show how we were conditioned. Not conditioned by the Communists, but by a general civic conditioning, in the years 44-45-46. We lived in it. It was the atmosphere of post-resistance. The time when I read Michelet's *Histoire de la Révolution française*, a book which left its mark on me. A time when one simply had to be "civic".

Let's not forget the formidable shock of the Second World War. I must confess that during the post-war years, it was the citizen that took over from the poet. I was probably not the only one at the time! We thought we were bringing about a new society. It was a task that took a good deal out of us, so that... I considered poetry dispassionately, it didn't seem to me essential, neither in a general way, nor for myself in particular. It was exactly the opposite position to that I have now; I was dedicated to militant tasks, the struggle for peace, for better living conditions, the battle of the book, etc. These tasks preoccupied me in a different way from what was happening in socialist countries.

In that Cold War atmosphere, I had chosen my side. I would listen to my comrades, not to our adversaries. Everything negative I might hear about Stalin, the U.S.S.R. and its "satellites" were nothing but old wives' tales for me. Oh, yes, I was a Manichean like Eluard, and I could say along with him (I quote from memory): "I've too much to do defending the innocents who proclaim their innocence to be bothered with criminals who recognize their culpability."

The innocents were victims of fascism and imperialism.

• *What is the date of the poem to Stalin in* Envie de vivre *(Wanting to Live)?*

• I must have written it about 1950, for Stalin's 70th anniversary, I believe. In the midst of the Cold War. At the time I pictured a Stalin who was nothing like what we have since learned about the man. How many members of the resistance died shouting "Long Live Stalin"? For them, as for me, Stalin was not a tyrant. He embodied resistance to Nazism, the struggle of the people of the Soviet Union, hope in the future, the "singing tomorrows" in which Gabriel Péri believed when he was shot.

Today, ridicule is wreaked on that faith. You will tell me that my poem was written in other circumstances, after the war. That is so. But Stalin continued to embody the struggle for the future and opposition to American imperialism. "U.S. Go Home." I do not laugh or snigger at those things. I really believed in the collective government in the U.S.S.R. My poem leans on my conviction that Stalin was a good man :

> For you have not kept your goodness either,
> comrade, for yourself.

So I did not make apologies for his crimes; I was ill-informed.

• *But in writing that way, was the requirement of the poet in you satisfied, or only that of the militant Communist?*

• To tell the truth, I realize that I went through a period of almost ten years in low water : I used poetry as a weapon, the tract poem. In *Gagner*, published in 1949, there are already poems of that kind. There are also some in *Terre de Bonheur* and in *Trente et Un Sonnets* (which have just been republished). All this must have lasted about a dozen years, from 48 to 60. I wasn't writing any longer, and I was miserable. I need to write. It's a mania, a vice. (I discovered later that when I'm not writing I can always translate.) I was writing, but when what is called inspiration, poetic surging forth, decreases, the critical mind also decreases. That is what is unfortunate. You have to be at your best to have a good critical mind. To create — I don't like that word — to write, to make something new and to criticize, to see clearly into what one is doing, all that is part of a whole. So that is the answer to the question you are asking me : I wanted first of all to respond to a political, let's say civic, ideal. I must have found those poems quite good because I published them.

I remember an anecdote; I am not proud of it. I was with Pierre Daix at a book sale. It was in the XIVth arrondisement. Some young people came over to me to talk about *Terraqué*. They had taken photographs of stones and ferns to illustrate my book, and I said to them : "Yes, your photographs are interesting, but I am far from *Terraqué*; I can't recognize myself in it any longer." In short, this book, that I was judging with the vision of a good-willed petit bourgeois, seemed to me like art for art's sake. Today I find that reaction astonishing. *Terraqué* is my foundation, my base. But without this memory, I would not know that I had been like that.

Back to my poem *To Stalin*. Of course I would no longer write that. As a poem, it's not too bad, but it isn't true. At the time, we put down any deficiencies in the countries of the Eastern block to ignorance, sabotage, and the lingering effects of former régimes. That shows how terrible were the revelations of the XXth congress of the Communist Party of the USSR and principally the discovery of Stalin's crimes. I was stunned for months and months. I am still not sure that I have got over it. My political convictions have not changed essentially, but the enthusiasm...

I have been told that I was naive. Sometimes I would reply that I had had the faith of an old Breton priest. Since then, I have come to the conclusion that I should mistrust myself in everything concerning politics, and that in any case I was a poet rather than a man of action.

I had often said in the post-war years, and André Frénaud remembers it: "Poetry is the enemy. It monopolizes and impedes immediate action." I have had to be convinced of the opposite: poetry was not the enemy, it was essential for me, the incarnation of what is essential. Without it, where are the criteria for action?

I remained a militant, but I had to find my field. At this point, I would like to quote the poem "Cherry tree" :

You have become
what was dreamed of,

only this whiteness
frightening the horizon,

only the fiancée
ready for marriage.

Who will take you ,
Who is to come ?

• *I follow, and I would like to keep quiet, but these facts, and
the numbing of your deepest nature, require some form of
explanation.*

• I explain that by the abandonment, or falsification of the
self, when one is no longer in touch with one's labyrinths. A
maimed tree, grafted the wrong way.

• *Don't you think, nowadays, that if you had lived out your
own longing as a poet, you would also have done more for
others?*

• It's as clear as daylight now. But allow me to think that I
have made up, and am still making up, for lost time. In a sense,
the experience is positive, because it has contributed to self-
revelation, and it works like a vaccine.

• *But how could that happen?*

• There was a kind of guilty conscience at still being alive;
we would think about all those who had died (at the time I had
not recognized all of that). Then also in my case I had the feeling
that I had not done enough in the Resistance.

• *Culpability again?*

• Culpability, a feeling of duty towards others, immediate

duty. And a kind of embarrassment at taking pleasure in the play of words. As if it were a game! Probably nonsense, but many other people throughout history have had this feeling. As if creation were narcissism, and narcissism social offence. For me, this period is characterized less by a lack of contact with things and with life itself, than by a less vital contact, or a different contact, with words. In my conscious being, I had more or less made mine the phrase "langue de bois"[25].

I think that when a poet does not write, or no longer writes, a distance has been created between words and himself. I believe — I don't think it is arrogant to say so — that when a poet is dry, he has a relationship to words like that which ordinary language-users have. I was needed elsewhere. I remember having said to a friend one day : "If I have to give up being a poet, I'll give it up." I'm not sure these were the exact words I used, but that is the gist of them. I hold nobody responsible for what I was all those years, but it is not surprising that I should have had recourse to traditional prosody. It was a rallying sign, a sign of submission to the collectivity; through the regular line, I went back to what had been taught me at primary school first of all, and then at secondary school. A kind of regression.

I went straight to the most regular, classical, constricting form : the sonnet. In every way it was a wager, so of course I was interested in it. Besides which I had read a lot of sonnets at school; and then, I liked that form! The sonnet has something in its form and its rhyme scheme that is right for narcissism. You become enclosed in it, as in a shell.

I have already asked psychoanalysts to try and see whether this explains why the sonnet, of all the fixed forms in French poetry, is the only form to have survived. Victor Hugo did not sacrifice to the sonnet. Greatness does not allow itself to become entangled.

One factor which probably played a part in the return to the regular line — though its importance has been exaggerated — was the influence of Aragon. At the time, Aragon wrote articles in favour of regular forms and he showed that towards the end of his life Eluard tended to use them. As I was going through a bad patch because I was not writing, I thought I might try my hand. It must be remembered that at the time I was doing a lot of translation and especially verse from the past — that is to say, in regular forms. Nevertheless, it was said that I had written those sonnets under the orders, at the instigation, under the command, of Aragon. It was even said in the Party press! What notion of Party did those communists have, then? I repeat, I have never obeyed orders received as such. I obeyed those I thought I was giving myself. I have said why I did so, for personal reasons, reasons concerning my life. It was after that that Aragon got on my hobby horse; I didn't get on his. It was he who found that interesting, and he told me he wanted to write a preface to my collection of poems; it was he who sang the praises of the sonnet. Aragon is a polemicist, a fighter. He found something there which was useful for a cause he was defending at the time; only afterwards he said to me: "Surely you're not going to write sonnets all your life!..." That is the true story.

Those sonnets were in general not very well-received, neither by people in favour of this form nor by others. It is not my poetry, it is not my voice, but it is all the same a certain "me"; I do not deny it. I have been this Simplicius Simplicissimus. I change, but I have no mania for denials : probably still a certain narcissism.

Between *Trente et Un Sonnets* and *Carnac*, from 1954 to 1960, I delved into translation. In fact I began much earlier, but in a much less systematic way, at about the age of twenty. That was when I translated works by my friend, the poet from Alsace, Nathan Katz, in particular a long story, *Histoire d'un matou*, a delightful story from a village in the Sundgau. I did not translate Katz's texts written in German, but those written in Alemannic, for they seemed more powerful, and translating them was interesting because of the nature of the original language.

From time to time it would take my fancy to translate a German poet : Goethe, Lenau, Hölderlin, and particularly Trakl. I still have somewhere some of these translations which I have not yet finished. For example, I have been carrying round inside me for about fifty years the translation of a poem by Trakl : *An den Knaben Elis.* [26]

I believe it was in 1953 that I was sounded by Ladislas Gara, Paris correspondent for the Hungarian press, and who had been living in Paris since 1920. It concerned working with him on some translations from the Hungarian, and translating into French some poems by Attila Joszef. Gara was pleased with the result, and we maintained a regular collaboration on different poets. I explained how we worked in the preface to the volume *Mes poètes hongrois.* I think we managed to be a two-person translator. Gara did this kind of work with many other French poets, especially for his *Anthologie de la poésie hongroise* which was published at the Editions du Seuil. As for me, I went on translating with other Hungarians, who were familiar with two languages and two poetries — in particular with poets and especially with György Somlyo — and my translations were put into the above-mentioned collection, published in the Editions Corvina, in Budapest.

I continued this experience — I still do — with Portuguese, Rumanian, Vietnamese, Dutch, Russian, Macedonian and Finnish (and so on) poets. I have translated on my own Brecht's *Baal, Mother Courage,* and many of Brecht's poems that appeared in the Edition de l'Arche 's publication of Brecht's works.

I usually say that translating poems is not difficult, it is quite simply impossible, and that human beings have never been successful except in what is impossible (transmitting sound and image at a distance, for example, walking on the moon...) and been ineffectual in what is possible (doing away with hunger in the world, and wars...)

In the preface to *Mes poètes hongrois,* I spoke of the technique of translation. Anyone interested can read it. I will just add that I recommend that young poets should translate poetry. It's an excellent school, a rewarding exercise which holds a danger: that of becoming too smart in handling words! The poet has the kind of relationship with words that people usually have with cats, coy in their dignity. Too much skill makes one behave with words like the master behaves with a dog! Skilled work, yes; virtuosity, no.

• *Have you also been translated?*

• Yes, into about fifty languages (books, anthologies, reviews), although it is practically impossible to know for sure. One occasionally finds out that one has been translated into Hindi, Bengali, Kirhhiz, Tartar, Chinese or Turkish... and when you think that in the USSR[27] there are more than a hundred languages... I must have a good score of books published abroad : two in German, two in Macedonian, one in Czech, one in Slovak, one in Polish, a Penguin in English, four in American English, two in Japanese, two in Italian, one in Russian; in Hungarian I have three: two in Hungary and one in Romania. Other books are in preparation, in Finnish, in Spanish, in Arabic. So I think I have been translated into all the languages of Europe including Alemannic, Occitan and Breton.

Of all these translations, only those which I have been able to read and understand — in German, Alemannic and English — have taught me something about my poetry; it concerns my way of using words. I realized how difficult it was for translators to find the equivalent of apparently very simple words. It helped me to understand that my relationship with words was not a relationship of *amour courtois.*

I cannot conceive of writing a poem without proceeding with caution. The poem is a response which sounds one out. That is even truer of the poem in free verse. The regular line, by definition, lends itself far less to feeling one's way and therefore to questioning. I know that because I have used both types of versification.

I have by no means published everything I have written in regular lines! I have written so much in this form, in particular some fifty poems about animals, written between 1956 to 1957, after the revelation of Stalin's crimes. Here is one of those little poems :

Je comprends que Mallarmé
T'ait sacré symbole, cygne,
De son rêve mal armé
Contre un monde qui l'assigne. [28]

As for rhyming, it rhymes! The world assigned me too. and I
was in the dark. To whom was I to address my *De profundis?*

And then one fine day — and the adjective is appropriate —
I began to write poetry again that was really mine, like the kind I
used to write. Once again I found my source, my roots. This
poem *Chemin*, which is the opening poem in the collection called
Sphere, is dedicted to André Frénaud[29]. He was one of thse
friends — Marcel Arland too — who helped me to be conscious
of my aberration.

After *Chemin*, I completely abandoned classical versification
and the inspiration that goes with it, as form and content are one.
Then I wrote the poems in *Sphere* and *Carnac*. *Carnac* was a
great joy for me, a deliverance. I found myself completely, I
found my country again, the land, the sea, I relived what I had
been before. Strangely enough, I wrote some pages of *Carnac* in
the port of Ajaccio. I was looking at the Mediterranean, and the
difference between that and the ocean must have inspired me.
But I had begun to write in Paris. It was triggered off by my
reading a text by Gaétan Picon on Mallarmé. He spoke of the
drop of nothingness that the sea is missing, and this reminder
gave me a shock, and I re-experienced the water of the ocean and
I wrote :

Sea at the edge of nothingness,
mingling with nothingness,

so as to savour the sky,
the beaches, the rocks,
so much the better to welcome them.

Carnac was off to a start, and I did not know that these five lines were the beginning of a book, and that the opening was there. I was delving back into the sacred.

The role of the poet, I believe, is to make it possible to live what is sacred. One might almost say that poetry and the sacred are one and the same thing. The sacred has always to be re-invented. And because the poet is a language person, he or she has a privileged role in this perpetual invention. In particular it is up to the poet to base society in the sacred.

In primitive societies, there was no distinction between the sacred and the profane. Everything was sacred: eating, walking, sleeping ... Those people lived the sacred all the time. I think that monotheism created this distinction, and that is why we find a kind of uneasiness in present-day living, divided between two realities. There is an error of idealism there, in the philosophic sense of the term.

As a materialist, I invoke the sacred. I dream of a society that would be steeped in the sacred. In my view, the poet should help others to live the sacred in daily life. The sacred, that sentiment that exalts you, forces your respect, puts you   in touch with something that magnifies you and can destroy you. The risk of total joy.

• *Something like cosmic grandeur?*

• For me, yes. If the woman one loves is sacred, it is because through her we come into relationship with the cosmos. When she rejects you, the cosmos closes. If not, why is there all that importance given to love? That is what I call living in poetry. Living the sacred in one's slightest gestures, just as I said in a poem in *Sphere* :

to Simone

When each day
is sacred

112

when each hour
is sacred

when each instant
is sacred

earth and you
space and you

bearing the consecration
through time

you'll reach
the fields of light.

• *You enter the hieratic realm.*

• For me, a poem is a hieratic monument.

• *Do you have the impression, when you're writing a poem,
that you're participating in a kind of ceremonial?*

• Yes. It is not by chance that a series of poems in *Terraqué*
has as title *Rites*. When I read them to Jean Follain, he said to me
: "To accept or not to accept the notion of rite: that's everything."
Living in poetry will be when everyone lives according to the
ritual they have made and invented. Poetry is not something
reassuring: it's a colossal adventure. How many have left their
lives there, their minds. My weakness as a poet is that I do not
take terrible risks; I hold back, I want to go on. I have already
said that I have always wanted to keep my reason.
There are times, when one is writing poems, that reason is
probably present, but it does not appear, it is missing. Of course,
I know the feeling of living in a vacuum, a space which is not

space, a space which is not governed by reason, but is governed by who knows what, the sacred in fact, that craze for emptiness that is full and fullness that is empty.... but all the same, not for a single instant do I lose sight of the fact that I am reluctant to leave the shore.

• *You speak of "emptiness that is full and fullness that is empty." Is that a formula or an experience?*

• It's a kind of sensation of the spirit, if the word has a meaning. Why would the spirit not have sensations too? Is poetry not a sensation of the spirit? Of spirit-body-matter.

• *Is the "darkness" you speak of a sensation of the spirit?*

• At the bottom of the precipice there is darkness, I can see darkness, I fumble around in that inner darkness in search of light. That darkness is an enclosed space, a sphere. That is why I chose this word as the title of a book. I quite like that darkness, for even when I defend myself, it knows how to break down my defences. It happens in vacillation, somewhere something vacillates, reason topples, it is snatched up...by reason. Some of my poems were written in a kind of delirium; I only realized afterwards that it was delirious and I try to delimit things more precisely.

Of course, when I begin a poem, I don't know where I'm going; when I wrote *Bactérie*, for example, I set out on an adventure, and later, on reading it, I began to understand what it was made of. Joy comes from this discovery. *Bactérie* is one of my most allusive poems, where hardly anything is said so that everything, the vertigo, the vortex, cosmic things, can be felt.

But at the heart of this vortex there remains somewhere within me — if it's not in the centre! — solicitude for the poem, the will to write, the will of the *poiein*.

Water
in any case.

Before
or after the death

of bacteria.

*

The same water
maybe.

*

The same
in the setting sun.

Maybe.
*

The same water
before there was
bacteria.

Maybe.

*

Already the puddle
on the edge of the ocean.

The ebb and flow.
The bacteria.

*

In that water,
for the first time,

the death
of a bacterium.

The ebb, the flow.

The same water.

The same setting sun.

The same?

     *

What
opens, what
closes?

What if it were the ocean
that the bacteria

had found dead
in the rising sun

• In a way, *Bactérie* is in the same line as *Carnac:* there is the same awe that I try to express, with greater breadth in *Carnac*, of course. There is the stupor, the fascination with that vagueness, that enormous power, that darkness that one cannot master. (It is also without doubt that need for mastery over vagueness and emptiness that led me to Marxism.)

I am probably not the first to point out that the Bretons who live by the sea have the windows of their houses facing the land — have you noticed? It is very rarely that you see windows facing the sea — they usually face the land. People are of the earth, the sea is there, but at one and the same time as a foster-mother and a terrifying scarecrow. "The trollop", for sure!

I am a living example of a Breton born by the sea, and passionate about the intimately-known land. It has been said, too, that in *Carnac* the land was the man, and the sea, the woman. That's fine with me, but it was not intentional!

I can remember a remark Frénaud made when we were having a discussion at La Forêt-Sainte-Croix where he came to see me : "You get on my nerves", he said, "with your 'one', your 'that' and your old-wives' language!" There was a moment's silence, and he added : "After all, you speak in the name of those people of Breton stock who have never been able to speak." What a compliment!

It is true that I am attracted to common language; I do not follow Queneau's lesson to the bitter end, but I think we need to be interested in the way people speak, and not use academic language. There has to be a dividing line, or at least an intermediary line, between the written language and the spoken language. What is more, there is no such thing as 'the' spoken language, but spoken languages. We can't not listen to those languages. In *Carnac*, as in the other series of poems written at a later date, there is no preconceived outline. A theme emerges, takes form, and I write. It is as if there were fecundation, the egg develops apparently according to its own laws, and one day it comes out, and everything is over. I write from day to day, I respect the chronological order with only a few exceptions, when words are repeated, or clash. When it is over I am astonished to see that it looks, in fact, as if there had been an outline, themes recur as in a musical composition, but I am not sufficiently versed in music to make a serious comparison.

On the whole, *Carnac* had a good reception, and the prodigal son was welcomed into the flock. I remember in particular an article by Georges-Emmanuel Clancier in *Le Mercure de France* and also a letter that Bachelard sent me. He spoke of a poem on smells, and said : "The smells in Baudelaire's *Correspondances* are nothing compared to yours." As I have hardly any sense of smell because of my atrophic rhinitis, I found that rather too much !

117

In Carnac, the smell of the earth
is difficult to describe.
It is an earth smell
perhaps, but removed
to the scale of geometry.

Where the wind, the sun, the salt,
iodine, bones, spring-water from the fountains,
dead shellfish, herbs, liquid manure,
saxifrage, hot stone, refuse,
wet washing, people's old clothes, their words,
and forever the wind, the sun, the salt,
the somewhat shameful humus, the dried seaweed,
together and apart contend
with the era of the menhirs

to gain dimension.

This poem is one of the most earth-water poems I have ever
been able to write. Doubtless Bachelard contrasted these sea
smells with Baudelaire's city smells. I believe that *Carnac* is an
example of what I have called "living in poetry". Thus I say :

The herbs of Carnac
on the edge of the road
are epic herbs
undiminished by rest.

Living in poetry, making an ordinary object, however hum-
ble, become the equivalent of the ocean, or a menhir. Living a
certain degree of exaltation in the communion with everyday
things, a sprig of heather just as much as the ocean.

I was haunted by the land where I was born, and I had to say
so. We should only write what we feel compelled to write. And

one fine day or another — as I have said — the flow stops, the book is written, not finished, for the "perfect chemist" work that Baudelaire talks about has still to be done. What does that work consist of? Simplifying to an extreme, one might say it consists of finding the right word, but this simplification is inexact. The precise word can be looked for if what this word has to convey is clear and precise. It is not the case here.

Let us use for convenience the terms container and contained; the relationship between the two words is not only dialectical — the precision given to one influences the other — but the container itself remains hazy, to a certain extent, until the poem is finished : for we are looking for something without knowing exactly what it is.

The experience that gave rise to the poem has to be relived intensely, deeply, and one has to dig, tear, scratch into the fabric of that experience. The words, the syntax, everything that makes up the idiom are instruments of this work, and of course also the many memories and references that come from our knowledge of poets of past and present as well as from one's own poems. It is there that feeling, sensation and critical spirit interact.

One might think that the role of criticism is above all negative, and acts as a protection. That is not my opinion. It is through this work in which reason and ecstacy appear to repulse and espouse each other to the point of bringing about a state of stupor or anxiety, that an appropriate synthesis comes about — I cannot say it more precisely — between this and this.

Then comes the moment when one knows one will go no farther, that one can do no better. If the poem is truly "successful", a new clarity comes into existence. I will add that during this process, these experiments on these bodies which do not appear to the external senses, everything occurs as if the researcher had within him, in those spaces he explores, another taste, another sense of touch, another sense of smell, another sense of sight, another sense of hearing.

I have insisted upon the importance I give to a critical spirit and to reason in the task of writing. There is no mistake about it.

Their role during this process is not to explain and interpret. If during the making of the poem, the image of the blackbird and the word "blackbird" come to mind again, I am not going to wonder why this happens and interpret what some people consider to be a symbol. The sight of the blackbird, and therefore the word, command my attention; my critical spirit and my reason intervene to know whether this presence of the blackbird in the poem is properly integrated, or whether it is spurious or inapt. Work of a chemist, gut work. When the poem is finished, it sends you packing, leads you to the door. The Sphinx has become metamorphosed into Oedipus!

When I say poem, I mean the verbal unity (verses, lines and words) having a certain autonomy, even if it is integrated into a series of poems itself forming a poem. Thus the poem *Inclus* is made up of two hundred and twelve poems. I am aware that this lack of distinction is not logical, but I have never managed — and I regret that — to find different designations for both things. Since each text has that verbal autonomy within the series, I cannot call them verses or fragments; given the unity of the whole, they make up a poem. I only found a solution after *Du Domaine*, in which the poems are so short that I christened them *quanta*, referring to Max Planck's theory. Isn't a poem a form of energy? Energy destined to reach the reader, and the result will be... unforeseeable.

To give an example, I will mention two readers' letters which I find striking and which show how the poem is an incitation to something unsuspected beforehand. One of these letters, somewhat erudite and well-written, was sent to me by a nun. (I still remember her name). She told me of the joy she had in reading *Sphère* and pointed out : "When one writes a book like that, one can lie down and die!" (That was not my feeling at all!) She added that she was very ill, and had just had surgery for the thirteenth time and was close to death. She ended: "I shall die quoting some of your lines and the name of Jesus." The lines in question were taken from *En cause*.

The second letter also concerned *En cause*. The man who

wrote to me had read this poem when it was published in N.R.F. The letter was written on sheets of paper taken from a school exercise book, in awkward handwriting with spelling mistakes. Its author, who quoted some lines and commented on them, told me of the comfort he obtained from this poem in his particular circumstances. These circumstances were materialized by a seal "Fresnes Prison". I asked my friend Paul Chaulot, poet and police superintendent (he was posted to the Ministry of the Interior, in the Copyright office), whether he could find out about this man. That is how I found out that he was a man of about forty, caught red-handed with explosives during the Algerian war. This member of the O.A.S. had fought in the L.V.F.[30] wearing an S.S. uniform. He had in fact been a Nazi, and it was he who told me my poetry helped him to live.

> So great were the days
> like long moments
> chequered in space,
>
> so great when love came,
> tenderness, the gift,
>
> the song sung so high
> when they sang along with us
> the walls and the window,
> the twigs of the woods,
> the stone of the rocks,
> iron and salt,
> water from all springs,
> and the horizon itself
>
> so often was the song sung
> of the crickets dead with joy,
>
> so deep was the silence

where the song listened to itself,

that we reached
the highest altitudes —

or what was it?

Seeing, that is everything.

   — To know
that vision
is not sight,

even if sight leads
to vision.

But sight without vision
is our point of anchorage.

Simply,
seeing.

That does not seem strange or complicated to me. I said so in
another poem :

It is not hard

to see, in a tuft of grass,
a conflagration
where cathedrals are exalted,
to see a river
rushing to save them.

Not hard
to see there naked girls
snapping their fingers at the cathedrals
and dancing on the river
that sings of the conflagration,

to see the army come
spitting through its tanks
to acclaim its victory
on the back of the river.

— But to see the tuft of grass.

To see things as they really are, what they are in themselves, as far as we possibly can. We do not know how the grass sees itself, experiences itself, or how it sees its neighbour. It's a matter of seeing first of all like a camera lens and incorporating that sight in a current, an epic — I am coming back to that word — the epic of the everyday. No complacency with the fantastic. What interests me in this world is trying to see what it really is, what we really are, what we are in relation to things, and what things are in relation to us. I wrote recently:

Rave, rave
in what is true.

Break free of clichés as, for example, the microscope does[31].
    I will take the risk of saying that for me the poet is less a seer than a voyeur, and here I am referring to pre-Socratic poetry, when the poet was at one and the same time sage, thinker and cantor. When I hear certain scientists, I tell myself now that that synthesis is not eternally possible.

    • *Isn't being a "voyeur" putting oneself on the same level as things?*

• I'll answer that question with another passage from *Inclus* :

He wanted to be weak
so as to be inferior to
whoever comes
asking for shelter.

He became frail
so as not to frighten anyone.

He found his way
into the hollow
of stones, cities, people,
so as to know
what it's like
inside.

He opened up
as if he were but an opening.

He almost looked
as if he were always asking,
even begging,
to be on a par
and even beneath.

He became a blade of grass
at the edge of the path
to be trampled on.

But all this time,
he was looking.

He took back his own size,

he remembers.

Because he writes.

To write is to *inscribe* oneself in the world, and that leaves its mark on whoever is writing. I do not wish to say that each poem modifies the one who is writing, but it is true that had I not written *Terraqué*, I do not know what I would be. Just as if I had not written *Ville*, I would no longer be able to live in Paris. I wrote that book because I could not stand the city any more. At the time I was living in the centre of Paris in the Rue Grégoire de Tours, in the heart of Saint-Germain-des-Prés. It was noisy, and busy; I am not saying it was a deliberate act: I am going to write about the town in order to cure myself, but to a certain extent it was a conscious act. I began writing about things that had no direct bearing on the city, but which led me to the city. After having written and published this book — because for me publication is part of writing, we are not free of things until they are published, that is to say given over to others — I felt much better in Paris. I can put up with myself and I can put up with the city.

A further proof that writing is revelatory is the beginning of *Euclidiennes*. I wrote those poems because I had realized, on writing *Carnac* and *Sphère*, that I had within me some notions of mathematics and geometry. Moreover, I chose the word "sphere" as title because it was the one which most frequently recurred in the poems of that collection.

Euclidiennes is a series of fifty poems on geometrical figures. Probably elementary geometry, apart from the sine curve and the cycloid. I did not study high level mathematics. I tend to ruminate rather than to think, but at times I "conceptualize", to a certain extent, what I have been ruminating for a long time.

One day, when I was having lunch with my two daughters, I had a sort of illumination. I saw some geometrical figures, the circle, the square, the rectangle, with some poems under them. A kind of vision, for once! I wonder whether there was a real text or whether I imagined there was a text. Be it as it may, I said to myself : "It's fine, it's very interesting, all I have to do is write." Write poems about what are by definition truly abstract things. So I started off at once and I wrote the poems in the order in which they appear in the book. To my knowledge, it is an unprecedented occurrence, unless one counts as a poem mnemonic lines such as : 'The square of the hypotenuse/ is equal, let me muse..'

There came a time when I had used up all the images projected on to my inner screen, so I took up the *Petit Larousse* and found my inspiration in the figures it described, the rhombohedron, for example, with which I was not familiar. I must emphasize that it was the first time that I wrote poems with pleasure. (I can write poems with joy, but not with pleasure).

The book did not have great success in literary circles, but Maths specialists found it interesting, just as my next book, *Ville*, was more interesting for people in building and town planning than it was for writers.

Regarding *Euclidiennes*, there is a little anecdote — you know how I like anecdotes! I had read these poems to my scientific friends Raymond Queneau and François Le Lionnais, asking them to point out the mistakes to me. Le Lionnais showed me that I gave an old definition to the dot : the dot is the joining point between two lines, whereas today it is said that a dot is a surface reduced to zero. Then he made a remark about the last poem, *Diagonale* :

> In order to go where I must go
> I have the right to priority,
> I have the right of property.
>
> For it is necessary for two angles
> across the surface
> to have communication.

So I settle down without bothering
about less necessary plans.

"Do you know," he asked me, "the rule at the court of Louis
XIV about crossing rooms?" I did not. "At the court of Louis
XIV, only the king and the blood princes had the right to cross
the rooms diagonally. The others, whatever their rank, had to go
along by the walls." I find that one a good anecdote to illustrate
what Bachelard has called poetic reverie.

I have suddenly realised the relationship which existed be-
tween *Euclidiennes*, published in 1967, and *Paroi*, published in
1970. The *paroi*, the wall, is a vertical plane, and my book a long
commentary on the relationship between the human being and
empty or full space, with surface, and volume. One might almost
say that in *Paroi* I developed one of the figures from *Euclidi-
ennes* and enlarged on it. In this book one finds once again some
of the humour of *Euclidiennes* and the preoccupations I would
almost dare to call metaphysical. And there is always that
fortunate or awkward presence of the body... and of bodies, the
uneasiness or the comfort given to these bodies by the forms the
outside world presents. However, *Paroi* is denser, as if I had
gone through the Euclidian forms in order to deal with the
myth/reality of the wall. For that, I had to give more : if I wrote
Euclidiennes with pleasure, that is not the case with *Paroi*.

• *When we read* Terraqué *today, we realize that the books that
come after it are already there in embryonic state. It is as if
everything were there from the start, and only time allowed
things to develop.*

• That is probably true. We have just spoken about the wall,
and the importance of this notion has been emphasized several
times in *Terraqué*. But it was still only a matter of walls!
However, it would be wrong to consider *Terraqué* as a nave and
my later books as side chapels.

• *That is not at all what I meant. There is nothing eccentric or centrifugal in your work. I think, on the other hand, that all your books are concentric spheres.*

• I think so too, but I refuse to be univocal, monotonous and flat. *Enquêtes* and *En cause* are not in the same tone, as far as I know! *Du Domaine* is quite different from *Fabliettes*. And don't let anyone say that I am still writing Guillevic. A book like *Avec*, published in 1966, also shows, I think, those varieties of tone and approach. This collection, which follows *Sphère*, contains poems of tones and textures as different as *Donc, Gloire, Chroniques, Elégies de la Forêt -Sainte-Croix..*.

For me, *Terraqué, Sphère, Avec, Etier*, are stages marking half a century's writing...

• *Is there a time when you prefer to write?*

• I am not like Claudel or Valéry, who would get up and write every day at 4 or 5 in the morning, or others who write from eight in the morning to mid-day. I have no timetable. I was going to say: I write like everybody else, but I do not know how everybody else writes! I write just as well at night. I am a man of the night, and throughout my life as a civil servant I wrote a good deal at night. I sometimes write when travelling, in doctors' or dentists' waiting rooms, in an aeroplane, in a coach. Even in a car when I am driving: I dictate into a portable tape-recorder! The basics of the poem can occur at any time.

I write on small sheets of paper. My diary serves as a pocket notebook. I find it difficult to write on large sheets of paper, because there is too much white around the words and that asphyxiates me. When I write on small sheets, I have the impression that the oppression in the world is less important.

When I am at home, I also write directly into notebooks which are very often dummies of books, sometimes very big books. I have used, for example, the dummy of the complete works of Victor Hugo. It took me quite a while.

When I feel that the writing has a certain volume — I do not mean that it is perfectly finished , but that the poem is on the way — I copy it onto sheets of squared paper, always squared, which I organise into files. In that way I can invert, reverse, the order of the poems. It is in these sheets that I finish the poems. That is the work of the "perfect chemist", about which, putting the cart before the horse, I have already spoken. I hardly ever correct on printing proofs.

• *You always write with a* Bic.

• Always with a *Bic*, I like them! I am heavy-handed! When I begin to pace out the words, and note them down as if on a stave, I can feel the sap rising. I do not speak of inspiration, I use the word uprising — and why not insurrection? The word "creation" has been used, and still is, often enough. For myself, I prefer the word poiein. The word "creation" is not exact. Creation is from nothing, with nothing. A poem is written from one's experience, with words. (And words are not abstract things for me.)

To speak of creation is also, I feel, to refer to an idea to which I object: philosophic idealism. It is not spirit that engenders matter and forms, it it matter which engenders spirit, and spirit which, with matter, produces forms.

I sometimes wonder whether this notion of the artist-creator is at the root of the belief in the creation of a world by a spirit, that is to say, a god. As soon as the poet thought he created his own poem from nothing, he was able to invent the creation of the world by a spirit of which he himself was one of the manifestations. The poet was using more than a comparison, he was creating a metaphor!

To come back to what interests us, the metaphor is not, for me, the essence of the poem; I proceed by comparison, not by metaphor. It is one of the reasons for my opposition to Surrealism. For me, as for Jean Follain, one thing can be like another, but it is not that other thing.

It has been said, by the German poet Gottfried Benn in particular, that modern poetry can be recognized because it puts aside the word "like". I take exception to this definition. I do not say : "lips of coral", because lips are not made of coral. Words rise in rebellion at being metaphorised! In my work, on the contrary, words rise to their own truth. What occurs may be a single line, two lines, but it is always a tonality which is like the outline of a theme. Not a theme in the form of a concept or an idea, but a coloration, a change of fortune.

Something happens which is not necessarily the kernel of the poem; it might be the flesh; it might be the skin. In general, I do not know, or I do not know well enough, what I am going to say, I go towards something. I am unaware what the next line will be. I am aware of what I write at the very moment I am writing. It is as if I were a quarryman digging into a steep cliff — the cliff being both the language and the thing. After a critical glance to see if it will hold, I work further into the cliff, in view of what I have already taken out. And suddenly, there is nothing left. I am probably dedicated to the kernel-poem, the centre-poem.

After that, I put what I have written into files, just as one puts wine in the cellar. Certain poems will be madeira kept, others champagne kept, others recognized only after tasting them as they are! None of them will be "chaptalized" [32]. I realize that when I speak I use the metaphor frequently, while in my poems, connected to my labyrinths, it is, as I have said, outside my process of elaboration.

Finally, since I may take advantage of the occasion, I remember of one of my whimsical definitions of poetry: poetry is to appearances what alcohol is to fruit juice.

Alcohol ? The spirit of wine, for example.

> As far as words are concerned
> mastodons
> have little weight.

I began to write against lyricism. More exactly, when I

became conscious of what my own register should be, I took up a position against lyricism. Moreover I caught up with a certain mood of the times. I only need to mention the name of Queneau. I later realized that there is lyricism and lyricism, just as there is song and song. There is the kind of lyricism that is self complacent, and the kind of lyricism that forces the issue. Another image : there are greenhouse flowers and field flowers...and sand flowers.

I did not want to sing, it was the song that obliged me to do so. I do not revel in the song, but *moderato cantabile* the song brings me back to myself. Was it not my life's objective and was it not the caricatures of life that I rejected? On this point, I am indebted to Rilke, although certain of my poems were written to resist him. In *En cause*, I wrote :

> When song is no longer there,
> space is without passion.

These two lines are, I believe, a good definition of my position regarding song and poetry.

Song is, of course, a way of being. Living in poetry is living in song, and bringing the level of daily life, biological life, to a higher level. Therefore this song that accompanies life, that is life, is also a way of penetrating into silence.

Silence has always been vital for me; noise hurts me; physical silence, the absence of noise, bring me happiness and are necessary to me. (It is one of the reasons for my inadaptation to the city.) I have also always been attracted to the white on the page. By white, I mean silence. One of the poets to influence my writing, my making, is Reverdy.

I have already "defined" poetry: the espousal of word and silence. I have also defined it as a sculpture of silence. It is precisely this inclusion of silence in words that distinguishes the poem from prose. The difficult thing is making the silence be heard, making it be felt. I would even say making it be *touched*. I have tried to in so many poems...

I was greatly surprised, long ago, on seeing some very old country people, sitting on a bench outside their house, leaning on a stick and doing nothing. All alone for hours on end, they did not speak, and they appeared to be happy. I understand them better now. Old people have learned to love silence, they live their lives, they have learned how to be in possession of themselves, of the silence and of the instant. Silence is the vase into which the instant is received... I would like to live to be very old. To live that and see myself fading away, lucid and without suffering. It is perhaps an impossible dream, but I would like to see myself going...

Writing is learning to die, it is winning over one's own death, because in writing one has taken a hold on oneself, and one takes a hold on the world. That is why I write: to know, to possess, to take a hold on myself. And I hope to be able to say one day, like the Chinese general who said to another Chinese general whose throat he had just had slit by virtuosity of the sabre, without the former realizing it: "Come on now, croak!"

I would also like to manage to say like Fontenelle, who, when asked to come to table, said "Gently, gently, I'm not a hundred any longer!"

Alas! I heard my friend Jean Follain wish: "I want an agony"..., and he was knocked down by a bus in the Place de la Concorde. (And when during the night his body was taken to the morgue at the Hotel-Dieu, the night-watchman was reading Jean's poems.)

There's no end to silence. Silence has always been present in poetry. It has taken on a greater importance in modern poetry. But what is rhythm? It is the result of the suspension of the flow of speech :

> the long sobs
> of violins
> in Autumn.[33]

If I say : "the long sobs of violins in Autumn", there is no silence, there is no rhythm. It is because there is a halt at the end of the line that there is rhythm. Halt, suspension of the word, silence. In French classical poetry, there is the silence of the caesura, at the end of the line and between verses.

These silences in the line compel us to speak them more slowly. Modern poetry has become fully conscious of itself, its nature, its components. So it has given an important function to silence. I cite once again Reverdy, and I might also cite Ungaretti, William Carlos Williams, Trakl...

I find the case of Follain surprising. Through analysis, we cannot understand what makes his texts poems. There is no rhythm, there are no rhymes, there is no prosody, and yet... They are poems immersed in silence. Follain made a distinction between his prose poems and his poems in lines. He said that his poems in lines were more compact, more recollected. I think that if, in my adolescence, I read the *Imitation of Christ* so much, it is because it is a series of verses inserted in silence. That is also true about the psalms which I so much enjoyed singing. They are an alternation of word and silence. I like *The Story of a Soul* by Saint Thérèse of Lisieux very much, and I see her — under her shower of roses — in the lineage of Saint Teresa of Avila. When you think that a young girl of thirteen or fourteen offered God that challenge: if that murderer asks to kiss the crucifix before he goes up onto the scaffold, I'll enter the convent... (I would like it to be Lacenaire, I have very distant memories, they go back more than fifty years.)

But I still have the memory of the presence of that silence of little Thérèse. She was silence.

• *When you were a believer, what form did your prayer take?*

• An interesting question, but one that I have never thought about ...There is prayer and prayer. For years, my mother would make me kneel down at the foot of my bed, and I had to repeat aloud what she had made up for me as prayer, that is to say the acts of faith, hope and charity, the act of contrition, the "Our

Father", the "Hail Mary", the Creed, the "Confiteor", the commandments of God, the commandments of the Church, and the "Angelus", plus a few phrases asking for God's blessing on us. I had to repeat that every morning and evening in her presence. I am not sure it was prayer! I also took part in the prayers at church, with some exaltation on my part, but it is not what I would call prayer. For me, praying was not formulating phrases, but putting myself in communion with what at the time I called God. Prayer was that ever-available song of silence.

I have always been surprised at the difficulties believers experience in entering into communion with God. For me it was easy, and still now, even though I do not have the faith, I can have that communication without any problem.

• *Who do you enter into communication with?*

• With the best of myself, that is to say with with all of the other.

• *At present, your "prayer", not to say your contemplation, is the pre-poem?*

• The pre-poem, yes. That space full of recollection in which one feels that things come. Like everyone, I have said: "My God, let..." Direct, utilitarian prayer. I have said: "Forgive me my sins." I remember having prayed in the usual sense of the word when my elder daughter was at death's door. My prayer began with these words : "Lord, 'que faites-vous de ces corps que vous engloutissez?'" It was a ...

• *Larmartinian supplication!*

• It was also a revindication. It was in 1934, I was already twenty-seven years old and I was a practising Catholic. When my second daughter was in real danger, because she died at the age of thirty, I had already put aside the faith. So I was all alone to

134

cope. When I was a Catholic, was my God the Christian God? I am not sure of that. He was what God has always been, I think, for poets: not an entity, but a living being. The universe, incarnate more or less, in a figure. There was some pantheism in my Christianity, but it is true that I practised, I went to confession and communion. Is there any contradiction there? I have never minded a contradiction or two. I live, I try to live, in my own deepest truth, and let the contradictions resolve themselves!

It is probably in the poem *Déjà* that I have best relived my contact with God. I have never had Christ worship. What I found most moving when I read books about Jesus, was the suffering of the man, the figure of a man, but I did not experience Jesus as God. In short, God was for me that which rose within me from my own depths — that which, moreover, rises in everyone. On losing the faith (as they say), I dismissed the notion of a personal god. I kept my depths, deepened and magnified them. I keep on doing so:

> You will see in passing
> the smile of a child.
>
> Sum up for him in a smile
> what he is smiling about.

• *You publish your books under your surname. Today it is Eugène Guillevic who is speaking. Have you any hesitation about talking about Eugène?*

• When I began to publish, there was certainly the wish to be Guillevic and not Eugène. It was especially because Eugène was what my mother called me, and I did not wish to keep anything of my mother. So I got rid of it. The women I met did not call me Eugène until Jacqueline, who began to reconcile me with my name.

By getting rid of my first name, there was the wish to take away something intimate — an intimacy to which I took excep-

135

tion. At the time, I would not have been able to publish under the name of Eugène. Was I to take on another name? Oh! What if I had published under the name of Alphonse Marie Guillevic de Carnac!

In these interviews, I say quite a bit about myself, it is true, but since I have become a poet that some people appreciate, my attitude has changed, and I am no longer the humiliated, offended fellow that I used to be. Now I speak. Perhaps too much. Talking about my own way may help others to find theirs.

• *And you are surprised if people call your poetry fraternal!*

• I repeat: if my poetry is fraternal, I do not do it on purpose. I do not cultivate fraternity. I do not write for a social class or for any category. I write because I need to write.

• *Let's say that your poetry is not fraternal, but that you are a brother for certain readers, and there is an art de vivre, a certain wisdom, in your poems.*

• All poetry has an ethical base. Let's not forget what Nietzche said : ethics is dying because of morality.

As we are speaking of wisdom, I want to evoke the figure of old Vacher, an old countryman of the Beauce whom I met when he was about seventy. For me, this man was a wise man. He lived contentedly, respected by all and sundry, until he was over ninety-two. He chose to spend the last days of his life in a home. He said: "I've nothing to reproach myself with; I've never done anything wrong." It was true. He had set up all his children and grandchildren; he had settled family and municipal conflicts — for he was the mayor of the commune — whenever there were any, and for that he used persuasion. One day, one of his sons was not very pleased because his boy wanted to marry the schoolteacher. "You are wrong," old Vacher said to him, "because in the agriculture of tomorrow, a teacher who knows how to write well and add up will be far more useful than a farm girl." That happened more than twenty-five years ago.

When he came back from the 1914 war, he was in his early forties. Until then, he had stayed on the farm with his father and brothers. When he came back, he was the only survivor of the four brothers, and he himself drew up the plans for his farm. That man, who had only been to primary school briefly, traced out the plans for a farm that is still a modern one. He said: "In the Beauce, animal farming is done for; now we are going to have crops on a large scale and nothing else. We'll have machines, great machines, so we're going to need wide gates and lanes."

He had his poetry too. He used to go along the lanes and evaluate...He was a producer, but he knew how to look at a tree, a cloud; the beauty of things was part of his art de vivre. And that reminds me of a nice story about hens! One day he said to us: "We are going to see my grandson who has a farm in the area." We left by car, we got there, the grandson was in, he took us round the farm. I was very surprised, because having had to go off on my own for a minute, I found a pile of rubbish covered with bread. There were no animals on that farm on which only crops were grown, wheat and beetroot, as well as the mass-rearing of seven to eight thousand hens in four or five sheds. It was enormous, and the hens were standing up and always in the dark. They did their business on one side, and on the other the food went along in front of them on a beltline. Quite naturally, I said : "Cluck, cluck, cluck!" and they all replied "Cluck, cluck, cluck!" The owner said: "That's losing us a thousand eggs!" We left, no comment. Old Vacher said: "Bah! talk about concentration camps, this is one for hens, and those who look after these camps are no better than the others." And he went on: "It's the first time I've been to a farm run by one of my children or grandchildren, in which I wasn't asked in for a drink..."

He grew old gently: no lamentations, no fear and trembling. Rarely did he speak of death, and never of his own. He was serene, always resolute, always good-humoured. This man was a joy for himself and for others. He must have felt that happiness for a man is the ability to express himself, not through despair or boasting, but really from the depths of his being: now death can come, I regret nothing. I don't think I shall ever reach that degree of wisdom, for even if I am not afraid of actually dying, I suffer to think that death will put an end to my exploration of life. Until that appointed time, I shall be pleased to see what will happen tomorrow. What will happen to the earth? To the universe? Are we going to penetrate into the fourth dimension? (It's about time we did). I am thoroughly fed up with these three dimensions. My dream is that we manage to identify the fourth, to which, up to now, we have given a vague term: time. When we've pierced through that wall of three dimensions, we'll be able, in a single second, to reach a star that, at present, is thousands of millions of light years away. And I shall not see that...

• *Do you believe in progress?*

• I feel like answering quite simply: if there were no progress, I would have died thirty years ago from peritonitis.That's enough for me. Even aspirin is progress! I am a son of the Third Republic and secular education. I was brought up in the worship of progress...I think that there has been progress right from the beginning of time up to today. Of course, the progress in the control of natural forces does not necessarly extend to the area of morals.

You will tell me that the world is worse now than it was a hundred years ago. Indeed. We are entering into the technological era. We are in a period of transition. All periods of transition are difficult. For example, we put up with cars in Paris whereas Paris is not made for cars, but later on towns will be built in which there will be no need for cars, because there will be moving pavements! All that is a matter of planning.

I am not sorry that we can go to New York in four hours. I am not sorry that there is electricity and hot water in my flat. I have no wish whatsoever to go back to the times of the cave-dwellers, but this technology has to be adapted. The infra-structure at the present time is quite inadequate. Rentability is sacrificed to without taking into account the true needs of people. I think that people will always defend themselves and know how to do so. They will not let themselves be wronged like that. When the obligation for rentability is overcome, put aside, then we shall be able to build for people. For that, capitalism has first to be vanquished, because it submits to that law of rentability and personal profit...National and international monopolies do not think about satisfying the primordial needs of human beings.

Zero growth is spoken of as an ideal to attain. I find that abominable. When you discover the third world, even partially — I have travelled across South-East Asia — when you discover extreme poverty and misery, you realize that wanting to stop growth is assassination. How can we accept that hundreds of millions of men, women and children have no roof over their heads, not the slightest territory, and possess only the rags they have on their backs? Is it possible to say that we are going to let those people carry on living like that? No. We have to produce more, produce considerably and share it out equitably. That is only possible under socialism.

• *What is socialism for you today?*

• I am a Marxist, and that means that I have made mine the great lines of Marxist theory based on dialectical materialism, but I am not a Marxist theorist. I take Marxism for what it is: a method of the analysis of social relations (and even in this area, Marxism is not an open, or closed, totality.) So it is not a doctrine but a dialectic. For me, today more than ever, capitalism is ill-omened and morally condemned. We are all undergoing the general crisis of capitalism. I am in favour of democratic, self-governing socialism. It will be up to those who have taken part in revolution to find the ways and means to build a classless society in which the individual can develop freely.

What I am saying is improvised, but it is not my intention to give a lecture on Marxism : there are classic works to be read. At

139

the present time, we have witnessed attempts at socialism: private monopoly of the means of production and exchange has been done away with in some countries, but experience proves well enough that it is not sufficient to bring about social democracy.

I have no lessons to give to the men of the future. I hope to contribute to the edification of society through my poetry. A society is not only made up of an economic régime. Art will have an important place in the society of the future and poetry in particular, for it will help to establish new values.

That's enough of this didactic tone. I confess that I dream of a fraternal society (I am thinking of certain impetuses, very different ones: the Paris Commune, May 1968). I think that my dream can come true in a classless society. Is it, once again, a question of naivety? There is a great need for naive people like that.

If such is my position, it is not the construction of an intellectual. That kind of thing is well beyond me. If I appear to be having what is still a dream, it is because as a poor child, the son of poor people, deprived even and especially of books, I have lived in my own person the damage wrought by capitalism long before it was described by Marx and Engels. Without that dream, that projection of the future into the   present, this world would not be tolerable for me: the misery and distress of the majority of human beings, the constant threats of war, the triumphant display of money, corruption, vulgarity offered as a standard of living, etc. I can comprehend that all that makes the present unacceptable to those who have no vision of the future. I can even understand the temptations of nihilism, derision, the *Bordel à merde*, as Georges Astalos calls it. I can understand that the failures and crimes imputed to socialism are not absent from the present-day cult of derision, but do these failures and these crimes condemn Marxism any more than the Inquisition condemned the Gospel? It proves that human beings are not easily brought to perfection, but it also proves their persistency in becoming human. I understand it, but I reject it.

I detest obscurantism. As Marx put it, we are still in prehistory, and it is not easy to get out of it, less easy than we thought. For example, the relationship between the Soviet Union and China — quite unexpected for me — is a catastrophe and also a lesson of realism which unsettles one's hope to the depths [34]. I do not want to despair; it is too easy to turn back. If the way is hard, there is no other way.

The other way? The one prepared for us by capitalists and their thinkers. Their pharaonic society : millions of slave-robots and a few thousand technocrat-robots with their scribes. The proof is the development of unemployment, and the intrigues in favour of obscurantism. It might be said that the leaders of the game want to benefit from this end of a century and end of a millennium and create the atmosphere of the end of the world. As if centuries and millennia were natural divisions in time, whereas they are artefacts (contrary to the day, the season, the year).

• *So for you there is no ivory tower?*

• For me, that is not possible. I have not, or no longer have, the passion for what is political, but I feel that it is a pressing duty to show solidarity and face things with those with whom we share our anger and hopes. That explains the reason for joining the French Communist Party, in which a genuine active frater-nity unites hundeds of thousands of militants who are working towards socialism. This party is not perfect, we have swallowed huge affronts, but the most aware sector of the working class — the sector that is at the very heart of that exploitation and struggle — still puts their faith in it, and they always have. I am not arrogant enough to think that those people are making a mistake about their present and their future. I can be in disagree-ment on one or other point with the leaders of the Party and even with the way they act, but it is no reason to deprive my comrades of one of their own. I remain in the party, but I do not mince my words.

In May 1968, I did not agree with the attitude of the party and

I did not obey the instructions I received about not encouraging the recently-created Union of Writers. I kept to my own road of writer and communist. I lived those two months of May and June intensely, meeting all sorts of people, and participating in discussion; a communion, a fraternity, that delighted me. I never saw in all that the beginning of a revolution; I never really believed in the political revolution of May '68, but it was an important moment in the evolution of hearts and minds, a great poetic moment. Life became more interesting for everybody. There was hope in the air that spring! And the fact that the famous slogan of revolt and anger *"metro-boulot-dodo"*[35] was not just a spontaneous expression but a line by Pierre Béarn taken from *Couleurs d'usine* (Factory Colours), published in 1950 by Pierre Seghers, is not without significance. So poetry goes on all the same...

It should be mentioned that the status of the writer has changed since 1968. It was the Writers' Union that started the idea of the writer-worker, an idea which is fundamental in the law of 31 December 1975 establishing the social status of the writer regarding Social Security. Before that, the situation of the writer was like that of a mouse in an empty attic. Henceforth the writer has the same rights as salaried workers.

I realize that somewhere deep down within me there is that need for a "collective", an immediate communion with others. Guilty conscience? Perhaps. I wrote in *Douceur* :

> For there are killings all over the world
> and every massacre puts years on us.

Solidarity, yes, but I am solitary in my poetic practice, where I feel sharp, and want always to be. Others? Here is a *Portrait* :

> Hands,
> that's the acids.

142

Legs,
that's the standing.

The skin-colour,
that's the lousy food.

And the cough
that's the factory fumes,
and the dump she lives in.

Beautiful though; a beauty
that gives one courage.

It's the look
in those eyes of hers.

Yes, others: that working woman with the look in her eyes to "give one courage", that old landowner in the Beauce, old Vacher, so accustomed to organizing space, the city-dwellers with a public transport look in their eyes...

Whoever walks alone
takes the others with him.

Shows his despair about them
through hoping with them.

Among them are the countless people I came across in Asia, whose eyes also keep me going and give me reasons to hope. I mention Asia and I would like to speak longer about the journey I made in 1978: Tokyo, Hong Kong, Kuala Lumpur, Singapore, Jakarta, Colombo, Madras, Calcutta, Bombay. A two months' journey which changed my vision of the planet.

I think that flying over the North Pole, those hours spent above the Arctic Ocean, Greenland and Alaska, are an experience. You discover the fragility of life on the globe. It only needs a few degrees of temperature less, and everything is dead. It is quite striking to see a world frozen as if by something sublime. For the first time, probably, I experienced the sensation of the earth as a little ball in what seemed to me to be absolute cold. At that moment, I thought of the phrase of Villiers de L'Isle-Adam on his death bed : "We shall remember this planet!"

Immediately afterwards, as if to create an even better contrast, I came into contact with the islands of Asia and their great metropolises, teeming with people, swarming everywhere, noisy; it's not enough to have seen pictures of it, for you have to experience the powerful display revealed there. In this context, the professional economist is fascinated. There is astonishment at learning that for most of the people one meets, Europe is unknown, and France even less so. Astonishment at seeing men, women and children walking tirelessly along the roads.

With the exception of Japan, Singapore, and, to a lesser degree, Hong Kong, poverty is everywhere obvious but not accepted. In Bombay, for example, and especially Calcutta. It's quite obvious to me that the future of the world is at stake in this Asia of which Europe, and France, are but an appendix. There are more than two billion people there. India alone has a population double that of both Americas...

I met a banker friend, a specialist in the problems of the Third World, who said that in a few decades Calcutta will replace New York. Of course, I am not a prophet. When you have seen western capitals, you have a feeling of exhaustion; in Asia, what you feel is vitality, energy looking out for energy. Even cement becomes tropical!

During that trip, as my English is not up to much, I was often taken for a German, sometimes for an Italian, but rarely for a Frenchman! Long ago, at school, I was often taught about the importance of the French language. So where were French books? It is true that English is becoming the world language of communication. English is victorious until it dies down, because this universal vulgarization is breaking up and debasing the

English language. Meanwhile, English is driving out French and crushing it. I have seen many examples.

One of these was in New York, at Kennedy airport where, in 1975, the message over the loudspeaker was given only in English, and as I protested, other passengers commended me for doing so. For many people, even among our own compatriots, one is considered very ignorant if one does not speak English.

• *You are not always travelling. In Paris, for example, do certain places hold a charm for you, or if you like, energize you?*

• Yes, there are places in which I feel better than in others, soothing, anonymous places where I like to walk. For example, the Rue Hallé or the Rue Broussais. A quite deserted street along the Sceaux line and the Saint Anne hospital, where many people are afraid of walking. A small grey desert in Paris.

Follain taught me a good deal about looking at the city. I am never attracted to what is picturesque; I am not very interested in monuments, but sometimes in a wall, a shady place, the colour of stone. I am not on the lookout for sites. I am not a tourist. What I liked in that corner of the Beauce where I had the use of a house, was that the landscapes were unfinished. I want to partake, compose my landscape, my painting: a little wood, bushes, fields. In Paris I do that from a window nook...

I have my favourite places; for example, Carnac: Por-en-Dro, the lines of menhirs, the church, the Saint-Cornély fountain. I am alien to exoticism. In the Far East, I felt fine, I was at ease, whether I liked it or not, but I did not go into ecstacies over the differences. I remember having looked at the Indian Ocean just as I would look at the sea at Carnac. Deep down, one of my characteristics is that I hate being away from home, I don't like travelling... And yet the frangipani trees, and the flame trees...

If I travel, it is for professional reasons and to meet people, but I do not like moving around. Wherever I am, I look for what is essential in this world. And I have travelled enough to know that the essential does not depend on longitudes and latitudes. Staying in the same place, listening and watching out for what is outside and inside, has no end to it, and that's my joy. When I go to a new town, I do not move, I stay in my hotel room and wait until some one comes to fetch me. If I have someone to take me around, I let them do so whilst we are out, but, as soon as I can, I go back to my room and I read. (Recently, in Warsaw, it was raining, and I read Descartes' *Discours de la méthode* and the *Correspondance* in a very decent hotel bedroom.)

I would rather wander through forests than along city streets. I am not afraid of the silence of forests. Forest clearings are important places for me, for I like to have space, wide open spaces, before me, and discover the sky and the fields. I would not like to live where I can look at famous buildings or tourist sites, or a breathtaking landscape. In a little poem I wrote :

If there is no ocean,
you have your palm to look at.

That is something that opens up possibilities other than those of commercial "marketed" tourism!

• *When you travel, you refer to Brittany. So it is Brittany you carry around with you, after all.*

• You may laugh, but I still haven't got used to the idea that the rest of the world is not made like Britanny. Seaweed is more real than frangipani. However much I try to convince myself, the frangipani tree is just scenery, while seaweed, for me, is origins. That's how I've always lived, but I did not know it. I am so occupied with my inner Brittany that I have taken so long to situate; it was ever-present, hardly linked to a space, to geographical reality. That presence — that Brittany — had no history and therefore no past, no future, a more or less mythical kind of presence. I had to reach maturity before I came to think of the past, present and future of Brittany, region, province, country.

146

Since it became part of France, the fate of Brittany has been absolutely scandalous. Take the example of education: at school I was never taught the history of Brittany. We were told about the troubadours, but not about Celtic poetry. I learned about Anne of Brittany outside school — as if it were biblical history! No Moses, no Anne of Brittany! As if Brittany had always been one of those — inexistent — French departments. I found out that there was a great Celtic literature when studying German history in "terminale", and Richard Wagner and his operas were spoken about. For us there was no Broceliande, no Merlin, no King Arthur...the langue d'oïl (dialects of northern France) had been predominant for centuries when Brittany became French; and their predominance continued. Breton which was spoken by almost the entire population was not taught, so that it was broken up and diversified, and the dialect of Vannes today is not understood, or is badly understood, by the Bigoudans, for example, if I am to believe Pierre Jakez Hélias who translated *Encoches* into Bigoudan Breton[36], and who said: "The people of Vannes will not understand."

In short, the Breton language has undergone the fate of all the languages spoken in France, except for the langue d'oïl. It can be seen that after the triumph of this language, the important poets and the important movements in poetry (the school of Lyons, Parisian classicism, etc.) all came out of the langue d'oïl, with only a few exceptions: poets born in high society and who had learned French, d'Aubigné, for example.

That was so even before capitalism. The development of capitalism strengthened the domination of of the langue d'oïl, tending through industrialisation to centralisation, and so to the unification of the provinces. Under Louis IV it was already well on the way, and was of course accentuated and made worse by the French Revolution which did away with all the regions (the provinces, as they were called) and created departments which are factitious, and voluntarily so, for it was not considered expedient for the departments to have a unity. That was the fight against the Girondists. It was done in a higgledy-piggledy manner so that there should be as much variety as possible in the soils of each department. The Jacobin movement was a unification movement, which set out to destroy regional differences. In the nineteenth century, the authorities continued this. The building of railways under Louis-Philippe is a perfect illustration of this: all the railway lines from all over France are seen to converge on Paris, and there is not a single transversal line! It is also an illustration of the dictatorship of capital. Bankers had their thrones in Paris.

Thanks to the Republic and its school, eminent poets emerge, at the end of the nineteenth century, from the Pays d'oc, for example, but they write in French. I may be wrong, but I think the first of these is Germain Nouveau[37]. Today there is a renewal which does not seem to be artificial, provincial poetry, Breton in particular. If, in the regions, a movement is developing towards a literature deriving from them and finding its particularity in them, it is probably not mere chance might say that it is a movement of revolt against uniformity, the robotization of this period of transition we are going through, and of this world which is losing its humanity in and through concrete.

How far will this movement go? Who can say? As for me, I am in favour of a certain cultural autonomy. Must it be accompanied by political autonomy or be subordinate to it? It is possible. For my part, I am not opposed to that.

I have already been reproached with writing in French, in the language of the Occupier (this reproach has even been made to me by Germans and by people from Mahgreb); to this I reply that one should not confuse victim and executioner. I was not able to learn Breton, as I was not allowed to, and that means that my mother tongue is not that of my mother, and I chose to espouse the French language out of necessity. It turned into a passionate marriage. I suffer a good deal from the real threat that weighs down on the French language, but that does not prevent me from wishing that all Bretons, like all provincial people, should become perfectly bi-lingual. Then the poet would choose his own language. Would I have chosen Breton?

I whispered your name:
heather, heather —

as if I knew that later
I would miss you

and the sunset
which consecrates you

Empress in the rank of the poor.

Greetings to Corbière!
Corbière and Villon and Laforgue and Lautréamont and
Keats and Shelley and Lermontov and Essenine and Novalis and
Trakl... died before the age of thirty. They are among the poets I
have lived with. I fed on them. They helped me to live. They are
my brothers, we are always the same age. But I am also the age
of Goethe, the age of Victor Hugo. That also is living in poetry.
I can say that — from the height or the depth — about my
seventy-two years: I am in fairly good health, with a few impedi-
menta, like everyone else. I enjoy life, and since I retired I have
had no need to think about keeping to a schedule, or leading a
double life. I have all my time to myself, so to speak. But I use a
good part of my time militating for the improvement of the
moral and material situation of the writer, taking part in the
activities of ad hoc organisatons: Writers' Union, Académie
Mallarmé, Writers' Permanent Council, Centre National des
Lettres, etc.
There is also the contact with young poets: reading their first
collections... I don't manage to do all I should, and that bothers
me, but it would be easy to spend all one's time on it! Writing a
serious letter requires the concentration which brings about a
serious reading, so that any letter or any meeting requires time
which often is not available; even more so because I find it

difficult to leave my labyrinths and adapt to the labyrinths of other people.

There is also what is called Parisian literary life. It is often made fun of, but it facilitates pleasant and useful meetings. Sometimes there is a certain emulation. There is the international literary life, travelling, festivals, friends from foreign parts staying in Paris; and that fraternity in different countries and continents is essential.

All these occupations put together make a more or less accelerated whirlwind of my days, and I have to protect myself in order to have my private "parking space." Jean Tortel has said that on reading me you would think I lived a solitary life somewhere in the country, whereas in fact I am always somewhere between two appointments or two meetings. All the same, I have written and published a good deal in the last fifteen years. I still have a good many unpublished texts, so that I could live for another ten years or so without writing at all, and still publish regularly. I make mine the opinion of Czeslaw Milosz, a Polish poet living in America, who told me recently in a restaurant in Rotterdam that inspiration has been with him constantly since the age of sixty-five. I would refer to Victor Hugo if inspiration had not been permanent in his case from his early youth... Amen.

I have suddenly had an idea. I have already explained my use of the short poem I call "quanta". This form probably has a cause I had never thought about. I think that writing a long poem is often going out in search of poetry. There is no need of that for anyone who lives under a constant poetic thrust, that is to say in vibration with the world. Then the poem is no longer a quest, but a safety valve, the overflow of excess. It is allowing just enough to brim over in order to find one's cruising speed.

In short, my poems are precipitates in the chemical sense of the term, and to go on using metaphors I shall say, with a wink of recognition to Molière, that they are "blood-letting", and Monsieur Diafoirus let no more blood than was necessary. It is in this state of "gushing out" that I wrote *Du Domaine* from 1973 to 1977: a series of four hundred and six quanta. In fact, I wrote far more, at least twice as many, in a kind of fever, and I rejected the less valid ones. It was a curious experience, because for the first time I was situated in a limited space surrounded with hedges, and I did a job there comparable to that of an explorer, often astonished by what I was discovering.

I can do no better than to reproduce here, in part, the page I had given to the magazine *Création* (t.X) :

"One evening in July 1973, at the beginning of a meal at the restaurant called La Frégate, on the banks of the Seine (I was sitting near 'Montherlant's table'), some lines or something similar came to me :

In the estate that I manage
the wind is not mentioned.

What was that estate? I had never thought of an estate in my life (even though in my forty years as a civil servant in the Ministry of Finance I often happened to use the expression "in the estate of...". Was it the beginning of a poem? Probably not. Rather the first poem or the first verse, or — what can one say? — the first quanta of a long series of similar poems, because for quite a while, something had been rising within me, and this something had just, perhaps, found its opening and was compelling recognition in its form. So one had to go on exploring this estate, and knowing what it was about. And the second quanta came, very short:

The pool

Then :

The role of sentinel
is given to trees.

The following night, I wrote about forty quanta. Always very short, a line, two lines, three lines, themselves very short. After that, I knew no more about the estate. What was dictated to me was hardly revealing, at least on the periphery of the matter in hand. The few people to whom I read the beginning were surprised (and so was I). There was a suspense there. What life, what living, did this estate reveal? A friend told me it was death. Hardly likely. And I went on with my exploration day after day, sometimes writing a few quanta or a large number of quanta, ceasing to do so for weeks or months at a time, and then continuing my quest. Or rather, it was the latter which required and obliged me to abandon everything and go, once again, to see the pool, the pathways, trees, animals, etc.

Meanwhile, I wrote many other poems, in different tones, some of them very light, like the Fabliettes, *but the estate kept coming back and taking hold of its manager. Up to now, I have written more than four hundred quanta, and I am still unable to say where it is. I have given up trying to define it. It is an atmosphere, a tonality, based on childhood memories which the adult refines through love and criticism. People will say that it is once again and in any case typically Guillevic. I can do nothing about that. I write like that because I cannot write in any other way. However, I think that in this area there is something new. I am only sorry not to be able to say what it is.*

What I notice is that the more I go on, the more the poem seems to me to have the nature of a flash of lightning. In the case of Valéry, the first line was given to him. For me (and once again, increasingly so), it is the poem which is given. A flash of lightning over the ocean. The image of lightning is exact. One can see, one can touch, one can feel, in dazzling light. This does not mean, heavens above, that what is written down at the time of the flash of lightning , does not have to be worked at; the flash of lightning is given, but not its translation into modern French."

I might add that the final quanta of *Du Domaine,* from

Beware.
Appearances
can be true.

were written, or more exactly dictated, in that same restaurant in which, as in July 1973, we dined one evening in June 1976; those lines were not touched up.

As I have said, while I was writing *Du Domaine*, I wrote "different" poems, *Fabliettes, Contes et Nouvelles, Bergeries, Dialogues*. I also finished the collection published in 1979: *Etier*, which groups the poems written from 1965 to 1975. (This book was to be published before *Du Domaine* in a book-club edition, but the club had to give it up).

I have observed with great astonishment that the word "étier"[38] is little known; however it belongs to the same family as *été, étiage, estuaire*; it designates the narrow channel that takes seawater to the salt-marshes. The one at Carnac always interested and intrigued me: that almost still water which, at first clear, would become thick with algae and minute living creatures. It would be swarming with life. Where did that life come from?

Is not the poet the channel that receives all that he can from the world and retains from it those little piles of salt : poems?

• *In a certain sense, as Etiemble has said,* Etier *is an ecological poem; in it you speak mainly of elements of nature which are more or less threatened. Have you no wish to face political and social reality in this topsy-turvy world, in a poem?*

• Yes, I have already told a political leader that if I were Victor Hugo, I would write *La Légende des siècles, Dieu* and the great final works! All the same, for years I have dreamt of writing a long poem like *Inclus* or *Paroi* about what is happening in the world.

It would not of course be a matter of coming back to the tract poem, but to go on to something, let's say, epic. It is an enormous ambition, but the result is zero. It is true that I am not a thinker, and I am not going to put into verse more or less abstract and woolly ideas with a hint of vague humanism. It is also true that the form to which I am irrevocably attached lends itself very little, a priori, to this type of undertaking, but these considerations are not final. Proof of that is a series of quanta recently written about the massacres. That's how the situation remained. Nothing else has taken shape since then, for it is certainly a matter of taking shape. I do not wish to enforce this embodiment through writing. I suffer and wait.

Even if you do not think
of those massacres,

they chew you up.

*

Dead flesh
does not keep,

it soon sets free
its component parts,

as if relieved.

For three years now, I have been writing an already long series of quanta, but which, in contrast to the quanta of *Du Domaine,* are in principle independent. All that is work in process, and it is difficult for me to say more about it.

What is new is that from time to time I use the dictionary to write or to bring about these quanta — the *Petit Larousse* or the *Robert.* I go through the pages of these books, and sometimes I have to look at several pages, and other times I immediately come across a word which I would never have thought about for a poem without a dictionary, a word that makes circles in the water, and awakens memories and sensations and feelings, and then I write "things" such as :

The candelabra
enjoy greeting

or

Place sometimes a diaeresis
on your instants.

For the first time in my life too, I am obsessed with the stars:

Fear
is perhaps not foreign

to the interstellar cold,

to the speed
of light .

*

In this space
beyond space

I call out to no one.

Listen harder :
silence is yelling
in the interstellar regions.

It yells
and I am part of it.

In reality, I am in the midst of chaos, but isn't the dictionary that which most resembles chaos? I love dictionaries, they are perhaps my favourite reading. I never get bored reading the *Littré* of course, but also the *Petit Larousse*. To begin with, I always learn something, and I love learning, there are so many words unknown and ill-known. Unfortunately, I do not remember them all!

If I were asked — classic question — what book would you like to take on a desert island? If I could only choose one book, I would choose the *Petit Larousse*, because I would be sure never to get bored. As I have never done either Greek or Latin, I have often had recourse to etymological dictionaries so as to know the semantics of the words better. (I think I have already said that after I wrote *Terraqué*, I looked up the etymology of all the words I had used.)

But is it words that we find in the dictionary? It is their skeleton, their cover, not their pulp. I find that for many words the definitions given are not only different but often contradictory. One day, some examples of this should be shown, because some of them are amazing. This proves that words have no meaning outside the context. So words, which for me are living creatures, a kind of animal with feathers, spikes, hair, life, are, in the dictionary, like taxidermists' animals. They have to be taken out of it to handle, weigh up, force them a little, make them go into the poem and give them life. Then they find plenitude of meaning, at least for me, often violating somewhat that of the dictionary. As Desnos would say : "One has to raise the degree of the equation".

I believe all my poetry is thus made from a certain play at the frontier of the meaning of words. Using a word, not with the opposite or even somewhat different meaning, but encouraging it to be different, straddling its limits. That does not mean inflation, just the opposite; I am very much in favour of understatement. Isn't understatement a way of being rather than a means of expression?

> Words, words
> will not be handled
> like catafalques.
>
> And every language
> is foreign.

Foreign, yes, because words are not made for the use they have in the poem. It's the work of the poet that makes the word "wardrobe" have sap.... I am taking up my metaphors again. Finally, words for me are mammals more or less, and it is through torturing-stroking them that we manage to make them say something different from what they would commonly say, by themselves.

What I feel in the world, I have been able to put into words. When the thing is not written, in the strongest sense of the term — I do not mean drafted — things do not exist.

> The town is like a word
> I don't know.

The fact that words are placed on a stave like musical notes makes silence present to me, and against the background of this silence the thing stands out.

I remember — just a little anecdote — from my early childhood. How old was I? Probably under ten. My father said to my mother: "I have seen the mayor".(J'ai vu le maire). My mother asked : "The mayor from where ?" (Le maire d'où?) My father, pretending to be serious, replied : "Can't you be polite and say : 'The mayor of...' (le maire de...) Then I went off to reflect on the difference between "merdeux" and "merdoux". "Merdeux", elegant, "merdou", rude.

I don't know that it was after this event, but I remember that as a small child I was obsessed with words and numbers. At night, I would speak out loud, speak in my sleep, and my mother would say that I put words and numbers together and did additions, subtractions, multiplications, strings of words and numbers. Later I was good at mental arithmetic. I had twenty out of twenty in the primary school certificate. And even now I am a great counter when playing cards. (If I am less skillful with words, it is because they resist more.)

Poetry is not only a matter of handling language, it is not only an exercise in writing, but a synthesis of what what one has lived through, the to-be-lived and the play-experience of language, as they say nowadays. It is the equation: living = language. If there is no living experience at the outset, if it is word-play, for me it is not poetry.

Nietzsche has said: "For the artist, form is a matter of content." It is in the measure in which content becomes a matter of form that form is a matter of content. Form is a matter of content when it gives me a kind of vertigo, the vertigo specific to poetry. An example of this are these two lines by de Vigny :

> Pleurant comme Diane au bord de ses fontaines
> Un amour taciturne et toujours menacé.

Speaking about my attitude to words, I have apparently only spoken about myself, but in fact I was speaking about the function of the poet; the poet's social role, even if he fulfills that role out of passion and not duty. Mallarmé spoke of "giving a purer meaning to the words of the tribe"; I will adopt that conception by substituting for the word "pure" another adjective such as "sensual" or "living" or "brawny".

I have said that words tend to go flat, dry, empty; I think that is particularly true of French, the language of moralists, thinkers, jurists. How poor it became after Rabelais through Malherbe, Boileau, Voltaire and the others! What state was the French language in at the end of the XVIIIth century? It was becoming thinner and thinner, and more and more paralysed. How abstract is the language of the great conventional writers! Even the language of a man as lively as Saint-Just gives out a rasping tone! The French language was truly in danger of getting completely lost, and it was saved by poets and prose-poets (Jean-Jacques Rousseau, Chateaubriand, Joubert). The role of romantic poets was determinant, that of Hugo particularly. He said he put "a red cap on the old dictionary"; but I would say that he gave birth to a new dictionary. And French became a living language again.

The knowledge of foreign languages in the second half of the

XVIIIth century and the beginning of the XIXth was far from negligeable. During his exile in London, Chateaubriand read the English writers and Shakespeare in particular. The German writers of the *Sturm und Drang* also played their part. (Here the importance of translations should be pointed out and let us dare to say : Long live Abbé Ducis! He was able to let the enthusiasm for Shakespeare enter France).

Another factor which should not be neglected : the feeling, experienced by some, of what was seething up in the depths of the people, rumination and then revolutionary explosion. It has been pointed out I don't know how many times that the French Revolution did not have its singers, as distinguished from the Russian Revolution of 1917. I think the reason is simple: the Russian poets of the Twenties had precisely at their disposal a living, vibrant language, developed by the Symbolists (a poet such as Alexandre Blok, the author of the *Twelve*, was he not himself a Symbolist?), whereas the French writers of 1790 were unfortunate enough to have a dried-up language, unsuitable for the expression of revolutionary ardour and enthusiasm. I can hardly see the tragic, Shakespearian fate of Danton and the march of Robespierre and Saint-Just, on the razor's edge, expressed in the language of Voltaire.

No doubt the French language once invigorated again found the volcanic fermentation of Rabelais, but it ceased to be the language of an élite of thinkers and moralists. In this language renewed by the romantics, one can feel the life of preceding generations stirring within it, the lives of the men and women of our people whose language had not been castrated by Malherbe and the Boileaus, as popular songs show. Yes, a language is not the work of learned people, it is principally that of people in contact with what is concrete. It is in their language that people dream, make projects, show anger, blaspheme, hope, build, and it is what they bring to this language through expressing themselves in it that they bequeath it to their successors. Come! French owes more to the builders of cathedrals than to the legislators of the sentence and the line. I may have said that

better in *Inclus* :

The dead
are what
the poem is made of.

It is them we handle
when, at the altar,
we order the words we need.

Words
are their substance
embodied.

They are
the language.

They
secreted, and chewed it,

throughout days and months
and centuries.

In the poem, we are in them,
carrying them with us
to apotheosis.

The poem is there
where the words stand.

In the hollow of words,
the dead.

Forest of
openwork columns.

A comment which has weight : as the poet is the man who lives the language "of the tribe" and his essential function is to maintain it, to give it strength (thanks to that organic link he has with all those who speak that language), since the poet is necessarily a "professional revolutionary" of language, he will always challenge established authority, because as professional conservationists of language, men of power use a fixed, old-fashioned language. It is not by chance that Richelieu created the Académie Française; he did so in order to consolidate and reinforce royal power by attempting to halt the evolution of the French language. Absolute power requires an unchanging language.

To say that we wonder about the role of poets in society! And claim that industrial society has no longer any need of poets! Yes, the French language of today's industrial society is becoming impoverished; a new graft is required.

If the country continues not to hear its poets, what will our language be reduced to in a few years? To the faded bla-bla of the media?

Democracy is a stimulus for language; language a stimulus for democracy.

• *Tell us, is this Eugène Guillevic, clever, over-clever, not clever enough? The poet in society is described as as a somewhat strange, absent-minded, ill-adapted being. What you say about the work of the poet on words and language, his need to "go deep into his labyrinths", does not contradict that image, because, working in the dark, worker of the dark, the poet is not naturally at ease in society. But he lives in this society, and must have the possibilty of self-communion in order to write. Hence the need for a certain cleverness in respect of this obligation. How is this contradiction resolved in your case?*

• In my case, I have always felt clumsy, ill-adapted. Physically to begin with — I will not repeat my deficiencies. All my life I have always had pain somewhere, without — with only two exceptions — ever having had anything serious. Then being aware of my ugliness, probaby due to my mother's judgment rather than to my own physiognomy. That, plus my poverty and my situation as the son of a policeman in an unfamiliar environment, contributed to the fact that I felt apart from the boys of my age, and, to take up a classic expression again, felt humiliated and offended.

Throughout my life I have used a good deal of my strength fighting against that feeling, and adapting, being part.

> Periwinkle, periwinkle,
> tell him so, foretell it to him
>
> it is not his turn,
> he will not be set aside.

(It is in the situation of this struggle that I must place my faith in the revolutionary movement.)

• *Being the son of a policemen put you under a curse?*

• Allow me to say first of all that people make children suffer from the opinions they have of their parents. I am not aware of the current opinion of the population about policemen, but I know what it was when I was a child and an adolescent in the country places in which I lived. There were no other kinds of policemen, and it was up to the gendarmes to deal with all the repression of fines, offences and crimes. They were tied down to the uncongenial situation of having informers everywhere. The relationship with the gendarmes could not be a normal one of trust. In their area they created a network of mistrust and even suspicion. As I grew up, I realized that my father escaped this opprobrium to a great extent, because he was personally very pleasant to the inhabitants, and even liked by many of them. The fact that he would go and have a drink with them and often paid a round, was very likely linked to his good name, but (even though with age I have developed the more outward-going side of my father) that atmosphere of suspicion influenced me deeply. It is present in my work up to my later collections, *Du Domaine* and *Etier*.

Crafty? Certainly not as a natural tendency, but as I have just said, I had to be, in order to defend myself. My mother's tyranny obliged me to dissimulate — and in the least clumsy way possible, because my mother was clever and capable! She forced me into sophisticated strategies and tactics, one would say today. Strategies which I found particularly useful in the administrative life. I use dissimulation more than frontal attack.

Of course, this necessary attitude, this low-down Machiavellianism cannot beat a deep-seated naivety and openness to others, which was imposed also by my need for communication. Is not craftiness what the colonised are reproached with? And they have to be. Like them I have my fits of violence and anger. That kind of smartness is not incompatible with shyness and fear. I know very well that there is no shyness without pride. I have never said that I was without pride. Not all pride shows.

Too capable? It is not always unpleasant to play when it is not a matter of honour. One can also sometimes have the satisfaction of putting into play the resources one knows one has, but which one uses but little, because the important thing is not there. It can be pleasant to play the innocent with both self-sufficient and incompetent people.

What I can definitely state is that this pseudo-cleverness is free of malice. I can enjoy playing as long as I do nobody any harm. Even playing cards, I prefer winning to losing! I have however been led to avenge myself more than once in my life. My way of taking revenge is like this : showing the other that I am better than he is and doing him every possible favour. Is that being too clever ?

One more word : I wanted to last, I wanted and want to be faithful to the most demanding shred in me. I have managed my resources as well as I could. The proof of my capability is that I would call myself a miniature Goethe, but in the material and financial area, Goethe got on far better than I did!

• *Sometimes when people talk about you they say : what a personality! What do think of that?*

• I cannot see myself, I do not experience myself as a "personality", and I do nothing to be one. On the contrary, I have always tried to escape notice, in particular in the civil service. Maybe I am more "natural" now, that is to say I allow myself to be closer to my nature.

It is true that I have some vitality. I enjoy a social life, I have always been full of fun, even in the darkest hours of my life. (For my solitude: sadness, gravity). When I am with others, I cannot stand boredom, and I do as much as I can to liven things up in the group. I love telling jokes, I know quite a lot, enough to fill up thirty-six hours of a journey from Paris to Seoul. I like singing at the end of a meal — my hit success is : *Du gris,* that Berthe Sylva and Fréhel used to sing, and I'm ashamed to say I do not know who wrote it — old French songs, sea shanties, and bits of anarchist songs that my policeman father used to sing. He used to enjoy life too. I was forgetting my main talent which is that of pulling faces. In this area I am unbeatable. One day at Cérisy I beat Eugène Ionesco. It is true that I practised a lot during my childhood. (Giraudoux was probably right when he said that the grimace was one of the forms of revolt).

However, I think I am less interested in myself than most people are, and it is not easy for me to speak about myself — in these interviews, for example. I do not find it amusing.

I have already mentioned my narcissism, but it concerns less my personality than what happens within me, which is, at least in my eyes, an expression of the world through me. What I find interesting in myself is the *étier!* [39]

In a little while, another portrait — portrait or imagination — of mine can be read, in the series called *Vitrail* (Stained-glass window):

So what has he done
to this universe

to dare
to give himself this joy ?

* *

The assembly :

He sits down
as if he were part of it.

Personality? Why not, after all? If one is to believe the
"Portrait of Guillevic in Eugène" traced by Michel Deguy in the
May 1977 number of the N.R.F., we find on that subject:

*"Who has not run into Guillevic somewhere between the two
poles? At ease in his genes, Eugène! In Toronto, stripped to the
waist in his room; at Lake Balaton "I have some good tobacco "
..., in Struga, Massa, Helsinki...more secret than he looks
(economist, Germanist, communist).*

*Listen to him breathing in, that kind of asthma, that quality in
tone of voice, more precious than you would think...*

(You need only a single stone
to think about it —

...

Forests in the evening make a noise
when they eat

...

Words,
are for knowing

...

And not to know anything
but love.)

I can see him getting down to work at crack of dawn, like
Archimedes, and the poem, utopic, rearranges what is at hand
and leads it far away (one says "to bring close", to serve with
a summons, "to compare"...); he obtains the symbols of
everything needed to make a world...

(We are building the world
which will give us good for good
for we belong to the world
and the world to us.)

...chunk of gothic beam, village pipe oven, colloquium elf,
emitter of poetic quanta whenever there's a break,

(Time that can change
Cloud into cloud
rock into rock garden)

cutter of light into four, quadrator of rounds into quatrains.

(The pane facing the cold
trembled for the beauty
the frost would make on it
before daybreak...)

How can one be a poet in society? It tolerates him only too
well yet it doesn't grant him status. *In that place, which at one*
time was that of the fool, the funambulist of whispered truths,
how can one keep going, *except under cover of elfin disguises,*
in this want of status, *in that imbalance cautiously made good ,*
by a hair's breadth, in the lines of the poem.

Keeper of who knows what
nocturne and blood

against humankind.

Above all he told himself
I am the fertilizer
needed for later."

• *Friendship has a place in your life. The joyful and saga-cious portrait of you by Michel Deguy shows that. Most of your books, we can see, begin with a dedication to a friend, often a poet: Aragon, Eluard, Frénaud...*

• Yes, for me friendship ranges from camaraderie to deep affection. I have quite a pleasant nature, in spite of my outbreaks of anger which I deplore. And there is loving friendship which plays an important part in my life. I never set out to conquer, but I try to enter into communion with life through another being. From camaraderie to friendship and love, this communion takes on different forms.

I might say that woman is everything for me. There is the woman I love, myself and others. Speaking of the belovéd woman, I wrote in *Magnificat* :

In you
the world is resumed
without being reduced.

I think it is a good definition of my relationship with her. It is through woman that I am best in communion with the world. A love which includes, of course, physical love, communion, the fusion of two beings. It is through that that I have the feeling of experiencing the world. Of experiencing the earth. At that moment, the void is full, and I no longer have that fear and panic which are the bed-rock of my life and against which I have always acted.

Woman is also for me a companion, gentleness, kindness... When one has been treated like I was as a child, cursed by its mother, one does not recover from this pain, but one's wounds more or less heal. I do not suffer from loneliness. I am always astonished to hear people, poets in particular, bemoaning solitude... I was so much alone in my childhood that compared with that loneliness ...

Many people, even those who have people around them, suffer from loneliness. It is not a matter of solitude but of non-communication. As for me, I suffer more from an excess of communication! I need to go into retreat; I need silence. I need to go into my burrow, and then I feel surrounded by the universe, filled with it.

> He does not wander through the streets,
> the streets wander through him.

Jean Tortel says that I live the life of God; let's put a little bit of humour into that. I experience the universe, as much a fly as a bay leaf; I live the life of things. Of course, I do not know what the life of a recluse is. If I had to spend a few years in prison — this hypothesis has obsessed me a great deal — I cannot say ... But I have not always had only friends around me, there were the barracks, hospitals, offices, etc. All the same, the wailing that goes on about solitude and non-communication surprises and annoys me. Is that egoism? There are many people with whom I have the impression — I may be wrong — that there is true communication. I can feel them, they can feel me, we are fond of each other, friendship, affection, camaraderie, love, all those things... I can experience a very strong friendship that lasts for an hour; an encounter while on a journey, for example.

It is often said that there are no love poems in my work. I say that all my poems are love poems. To begin with all my poems are erotic. It is always a matter of penetration, entering into communication... I have written erotic poems to rocks. I need to be in touch. Oh, there are no poems like those of Petrarch, but I have written poems directly inspired by a woman. It is true that for me love is part of sensation, feeling the world. I can write a love poem speaking about a skylark !

Living in poetry is living in love. I have known quite a few women in my life, and I thank them all.

I have never written a panegyric on woman, the portrait of a woman who would be the ideal woman. In a woman I love, I include all other women and I bless them as I bless her.

It is never you and me, it is always: you, me and the universe, or rather us and the universe.

I am seventy now. It has been a long stretch, but I do not live in the past, I live in the instant. (I am a poet without nostalgia; I think that is quite rare.) When I think of the future, it is of a collective future: future society, the evolution of that society and of the world, customs, people. Hence I situate myself in the present.

Some years ago, I was spending the evening with friends, and a business man came and sat down beside me. He knew that I was a poet, but he did not know me, and all of a sudden he asked me this question : "Have you wasted your life? I've wasted mine. I've earned a lot of money; one needs a lot. I've spent an enormous amount of my time protecting what I earned, and I have the feeling that I have mis-spent my life. What about you?"

I replied: "No, I don't have that feeling. No, my life is not a failure. I don't make a lot of noise, I have no bitterness when I look back at my life, when I look at it now."

I have had a difficult life for different reasons; I have felt physically weak, but that has not prevented me from reaching a ripe old age. My life has been hard, but I do not have the feeling of having wasted my time, of having wasted what I had, what I was born with. I have conquered, acquired, and kept. I've made mistakes, of course. I've made choices that I would no longer make, but I never hold on to regrets or remorse. That's how it is, it's over and done with.

Once again, I have lived life to the full. I have always struggled for improvement, but I have obtained improvement. There have been slips and setbacks, but on growing older I have felt more self-confident, less timid, less sad and abandoned, offended and humiliated — oh, yes, at the beginning I was — and I experienced myself as such so very intensely.

I have a passion for life. Like Neruda, I can say "I can assert that I have lived", I can assert that I have never knowingly done wrong, I have never been unkind. I have to reproach myself for errors but not meanness; I don't feel unworthy of the child I was at eight. That is of capital importance for me. I am not embarassed before the child I was. He could say to me: you have done this or that. I do not boast about what I have done, but he too, the eight year old child, made mistakes, so he must not exaggerate! I'm not saying that I don't blush before the ideal of an eight year old child, but that I don't do so before the eight year old child I actually was.

I have not lived for power or money. I have lived so as to share my life in communion with others and myself in a great love of solitude, but I have not lived selfishly. I'm no more generous than the next man, but I don't think that I have to reproach myself with anything serious.

I have made mistakes. Politically, I have made mistakes; I am not the only one. I have yet to see anyone who has not made mistakes in politics. Of course, anyone who never gets involved at all is someone who is always mistaken. Now my priestly sermon is almost over; I believe, naively, that I have written poems with stamina, sturdy poems that give something to other people, that can help them to live, and enrich their world-vision. I feel that they are likely to hold out for a while, if the French language itself holds out.

In short, I consider that if my life is not a failure, it's because I believe I have always been faithful to myself, to my deepest truth. I have sacrificed nothing to trifles, things of vanity or power. To use a now well-worn expression, I have really lived like a poet, I have lived in poetry. The main thing has been to have lived my relationships with the other — with the world, with things, with the other in the couple too. I don't think it is immodest to say that I have loved, and been loved. I have loved as I wanted to love, as I dreamed of loving. I have been loved as

I dreamed of being loved. I still love. I cannot conceive of life without *l'amour, la poésie,* as Eluard called it in a well-known title. That is what matters: love, poetry : they complete and interpenetrate each other.

Consequently, I believe the feeling, the sensation of happiness is possible. You need to have strength of purpose. There is no happiness without the will for happiness, without the struggle and the will to feel it, obtain it, keep it. Evil, as far as I can see, is sadness. Sadness is a moral evil which I cannot accept. Life is tragic, my own life and the lives of other people. Life is tragic in itself. Having to die is a tragedy. Illness and separation are tragic, but tragedy is not sadness. I prefer Sophocles to Musset. Life is tragic, so why don't we live it in a tragic way, but not sadly. Self-affliction is the worst of afflictions One needs to have, one needs to give oneself, the right dimension to feel the sap and voltage of life. It's not a question of grabbing it — it's not a matter for fairground wrestlers — one has to become very, very small in order to feel it. I cannot understand this desolation one hears about so much, a kind of vague despondency, as if life were not worth living. But the mere fact of being here, of touching a piece of wood, looking at the sky, feeling one's body, just having no pain, is enormous. Look at the moon beginning to rise just now in the sky ... Pity it doesn't last any longer.

I have spoken about happiness. There's a general tonality of life when we want to live it in happiness, when we tend towards happiness through the tragic, but this life is made of moments, days, months, years. One has to fill those moments as much as one can with joy — that's what I have done — with joys made of very little, of hardly anything. Once again, the feeling of existing.

It is often said that life is absurd. What does that mean? I am convinced that those who spend their lives living with others, for others and at the same time as others, here or elsewhere, do not find life absurd. I said with others, I also mean with the "other", this "other" including things, the universe. The absurd vision of the world robs words of their centre of gravity. The sphinx becomes buffoon. One cannot say that life is absurd except from a point outside of it. From what point ?

Is it absurd that a grain of wheat should have to truly die in order to give birth to a wheatstalk ? Of course, it dies.

From what point of view can one judge life to be absurd? We have substance, we are already thinking, acting, loving, writing human beings.

I understand why Satan judges life to be absurd. We are not Satan. We are grains of wheat.

Calm
as the lake.

After.
Before.

NOTES

1. Jeumont is a town in northern France, near the Belgian border, some fifteen miles south-east of Mons.

2. The word *Terraqué*, title of Guillevic's collection of poems published in 1942, is derived from two Latin words, terra and aqua. Now considered archaic, it is rarely to be found in modern dictionaries; it still appears, however, in the most recent edition of the *Littré*. An equivalent title in English might be Earthwater, but this does not convey the double sound-meaning of *traqué*, tracked down, which, during the Occupation, would have peculiar overtones.

3. Guillevic's book, *Inclus* ("included" or "enclosed") was published in 1973. Among its 212 short poems are to be found penetrating considerations on the art of writing.

4. Guillevic's expression is *tellurisme mystique*, a mystical attraction to the earth. I have translated this by the phrase "earth-worship", because Guillevic has just referred to pagan elements in Breton culture, to which, intellectually at least, he experienced a certain resistance.

5. In the French text we find *Dans Sophocle, on ne se complaît pas à l'échec, au malheur. Oedipe ne se complaît pas. (Sans jeu de mots)*. Guillevic is highlighting the necessary harmony between temperament and reason, and the need for integrity and rectitude in one's choices. Any complacency towards the irrational would compromise the existence of dramatic or pathetic elements. The punning referred to by the author in the original text is likely to be between the different meanings of *se complaire* (to take pleasure in/to be complacent/to wallow in one's misfortune, etc).

6. Lit: "It was during the horror of a deep night".

7. Marcel Arland (1891-1986), a French writer, was co-director with Jean Paulhan of the *Nouvelle Revue Française*. He wrote several novels, short stories and critical essays. He became a member of the French Academy in 1968.

8. Matthias Lübeck (1903-1944) was a French poet who, as a young man was on the editorial staff, with Francis Gérard and Pierre Naville, of a magazine called *L'oeuf dur* (1921-1924). He was a member of the Surrealist group until 1929. In 1944, he was taken hostage and shot by the Gestapo.

9. Guillevic had a great admiration for the poetry of Alphonse de Lamartine (1790-1869). Here he is referring to Milly-Lamartine, a small village in the vineyard-covered hills near Macon in the Saône-et-Loire area, where the Lamartine family had a house, and where they lived when the future poet was just four years old. It is in the beautiful countryside of Milly that Lamartine found so much inspiration, just as Guillevic found his own in Carnac.

10. In Brittany, the so-called "Pardons" are part of an age-old tradition, dating back at least to the Middle Ages. They were revived during the nineteenth century. They are large assemblies, usually beginning or ending on a saint's day, and lasting two days. There are two main aspects: penitential or religious, and festive. The actual "Pardon" or forgiveness of sins, is an indulgence granted to pilgrims. The collective aspect of this event, the "assembly", came to be an integral part of Breton culture. Festivities during the pilgrimage include dancing and singing: in Brittany there is no division between the sacred and the profane. In Guillevic's time - he left Brittany in 1919 - they drew very large crowds. Many of the pilgrims would walk a hundred or so miles to get there. The best known place of pilgrimage is Sainte-Anne-d'Auray. Guillevic also mentions the Saint-Cornély procession of oxen; this custom is more recent, dating back only to the late 1870s. It was customary at those times to clean the fountains to which Guillevic refers, and deck them with flowers, a custom similar to well-dressing in certain parts of England, in particular in Derbyshire. It is hardly surprising that Guillevic refers to beggars showing their stumps in a memory or "dream" he had, for this was a time when the poor and the maimed would line the ways up to the chapels, and give pilgrims the opportunity to give alms. see Yann Brékilien: *La Vie Quotidienne des Paysans Bretons,* Paris, Hachette, 1966, and Michel Lagrée: *Religion et cultures en Bretagne,* 1850-1950, Paris, Fayard, 1992.

11. "Terminale" is the final year in secondary school in the French educational system. Pupils are seventeen or eighteen years of age.

12. Nathan Katz (1892-1981) is considered to be the greatest poet of Alsace. Besides poetry, he wrote stories, an opera and several plays.

13.The Girondists were so called because the core members of the original group were deputies in the department of the Gironde. They were moderate republicans in the French revolution. They were mainly lawyers, merchants and journalists, fairly representative of the middle classes of the provinces, and they championed the provinces against Paris. They personified in a romantic though not practical way the ideals of the Revolution. They split with the Jacobins over the issue of war, and eventually succeeded in having war declared against Austria. After a popular revolt, 29 Girondists were arrested, several were put to death.

14. Here Guillevic is probably referring to Pierre Jakez Helias's book *Le Cheval d'Orgueil* which was published a few years before these inter-views took place (Plon, 1975). In it, this Breton poet, writer and specialist of the Celtic tongue, recounts his childhood memories, in particular the lives of the poor in Brittany in the early years of the century.

15. Judging from the period about which Guillevic is speaking, he is referring here to O.V. de L. Milosz (1877-1939), who took on French nationality. He later refers to Czeslaw Milosz.

16. Lit:"All those condemned to death will have their heads cut off".

17. Lit: "In matters of personal estate, possession is the right to claim".
  "Usufruct is the right to enjoy something like the owner himself, with responsibility for its upkeep."

18. Lit:"Substitutions are prohibited".

19 Lit: "We would no longer say/the bee pecks/ but all the same."

20. The letters C.O.A. stand for *Commis Ouvriers d'Administration*, who would be low-ranking soldiers in the French Army of that time

175

(1939), under the direction of a captain. I am told that this particular grouping no longer exists in military organization.

21 An agrégatif is a candidate in a highly competitive national post-graduate examination within the French educational system. Successful candidates are called agrégés.

22. The political crisis and tension of the pre-war years gave rise to very marked tendencies in writing: the right wing (Drieu la Rochelle, Brasillach, Céline), and the left (Aragon, Malraux, Eluard). Although Drieu la Rochelle had supported the Fascist politics of Doriot, he was ill-at-ease in this and in other groups offering different forms of political and social commitment, as Guillevic's remarks suggest.

23. Here Guillevic refers to one of his poems as his "trade mark". The foal is the trade mark of a popular brand of chocolate (Poulain).

24. The word "igames" (I.G.A.M.E.S.) made up of the first letters of inspecteur général de l'Administration en mission extraordinaire; used to designate a civil servant who coordinates the work of several prefects.

25. Lit: "wooden-tongued". In French the expression is most commonly used to refer to political cant.

26. In the original text of *Vivre en Poésie*, Guillevic gives his translation of Trakl's poem. I did not consider it essential to re-translate the poem into English here.

27. These interviews took place in 1980, and the remarks are to be understood in this context.

28 No satisfactory translation of the punning in the short poem here has been found, and therefore the meaning is difficult to convey. A literal translation is I understand why Mallarmé/ consecrated you as symbol, O swan!/in his ill-armed (mal-armé) dream, / against a world assigning him. (My translation does not convey the word-play in assigne/cygne.)

29. The poet André Frénaud (1907-1993) studied philosphy and law in Paris. In 1937 he became, like Guillevic, a civil servant.

30. The O.A.S. was a clandestine military organization opposed to Algerian independence after the failed military putsch of April 1961. It was notorious for its methods of violence waged against French government decisions concerning Algeria. The L.V.F. or Légion des Volontaires Français was founded in Paris in 1941. Volunteers were required to fight in the U.S.S.R. and to wear German uniforms.

31. A pun occurs in the use of the word *cliché* as a commonplace expression and as a slide, or a negative, as used under a microscope.

32. Chaptal was a French chemist (1756-1832).The word "chaptaliser" is used to mean the addition of sugar to wine before the process of fermentation in order to increase alcohol content.

33. Guillevic is quoting from Paul Verlaine's "Chanson d'Automne" . The stanza concerned is : *Les sanglots longs/des violons/ De l'automne/ blessent mon coeur/d'une langueur/ Monotone.*

34 .See note 27.

35."*Métro/boulot/dodo*". This phrase from a poem which became a popular song and is now part of the French common idiom suggests that there is little in life except travelling to work(métro or underground), working hard (boulot), and sleeping(dodo).

36. Bigoudan Breton is spoken in the region of Pont l'Abbé (Finistère).

37. Germain Nouveau (1851-1920) was a poet from Pourrières in the Var, near Aix-en-Provence. He indeed wrote in French. In 1872, he went to Paris, where he frequented Verlaine, and Rimbaud, with whom he stayed for a couple of years in London. He then broke with Bohemia, and took up a post in education for about five years, after which he left for Beyrouth, returning to Paris to live a most austere life. Most of his writings were published after his death.

38. The word *étier* derives from the Latin aestuarium. It is a dialect word used in the west of France and refers to a canal which takes sea-water to the salt marshes.

39. See previous note. The speech metaphor chosen by Guillevic is very powerful: the poet as channel or canal taking salt-water inland, to give savour to everyday life.